Word on Wealth Volume 2

Phil Dickens

CGM Publishing

publish this information is guaranteed under the freedom of the press portion of the first amendment to the constitution of the United States of America.

ISBN-13: 978-1516852642

ISBN-10: 1516852648

PRAISE FOR WOW

WOW, "Word on Wealth" is both eye-opening and mind-altering series. Never before have I seen poverty reduction strategies presented in such non-threatening, simple, easy to follow steps. This resource guide outlines the path to regaining personal economic power sieged by creditors and debt. I recommend this tool only to those truly prepared for the release of financial breakthrough.
-Violet S., Virginia

The definitive revelation of Word On Wealth is awesome! The Word On Wealth teachings will allow millions to spiritually and financially birth wealth as they allow themselves to gain and recognize power and control of oneself through the fundamentals of this book! The opportunity to invest in your books, Financial Bible, Foreclosure Assistance & Word On Wealth, has financially rebirthed and rehabilitated our buying power as well as we feel spiritually powerful and wealthy!
-Kimmi P., North Carolina

All I can say is WOW! This book has changed my life and I am grateful! The teachings are profound and God sent. Word on Wealth has made me go back and reevaluate everything I have been taught. I recommend that everyone get a copy of WOW, it will be the beginning of your new life.
-Darryl D., Florida

Table of Contents

WOW- BEING A DIPLOMAT

PURPOSE: To find the communication network and link into it

•Learn how to communicate effectively to all levels of people
•Learn how to present yourself and your message effectively and professionally
•Learn how to interact with police, judges, clerks, federal agents and other public and private people under any circumstance with success

FINAL PRODUCT: The ability to communicate effectively and present yourself in a professional manner to anyone under any condition.

Diploma. [Greek diploma – a paper folded double, from diploo – to fold, double] A letter or writing usually under seal and signed by competent authority conferring some power, privilege, or honor. Diplomacy. The science of art of conducting negotiations, arranging treaties, etc. between nations, artful management or maneuvering with the view of securing advantages.

When you decide you are going to jump into the realm of discharging public debt, it is vital that you know and understand the rules of the game. One very important thing to remember when doing this often dangerous excursion is that the bankers want you to know that "only they can use your credit – not you!" Of course this is ridiculous and absurd when you understand that you are the creditor and every product that you see exists solely on the fact that you furnished the credit to make it from the very beginning.

To start with, you should already be knowledgeable and effective in completing the administrative processes whenever you receive a dishonor from anyone of your debtors. These processes are detailed in COURSE – CONTRACTS. The key processes include your own private affidavit and the essential follow-up default procedure, as well as the notarial protest and the eventual involuntary bankruptcy proceeding to liquidate YOUR equity formerly in possession of the debtor. Notice I said YOUR equity. Everything the municipalities and corporations have purchased was produced by the use of YOUR credit as production capital.

We will be defining terms of all the actions and procedures relating to this subject. A complete study of the etymology of each word is vital for understanding and if done correctly the definitions speak for themselves in finding the answer. The following definitions are taken from Black's 6th edition which are typed in italics. The derivations are taken from the Consolidated Webster Encyclopedic Dictionary 1939 edition. The Hebrew and Greek definitions are taken from the Strong's Exhaustive Concordance to the King James Bible.

We will start with one of the most powerful terms on this subject that is the key to understanding redemption. Power of acceptance. Capacity of offeree (you), upon acceptance of terms of offer, to create binding contract.

Dishonor. To refuse to accept

When you understand the "power of acceptance," then you will see the world in a different light. You will realize, possibly for the first time that you no longer have to "fight," "deny," or "argue" as these are all dishonor. And, that you have the power to create a binding contract on YOUR terms. You will realize that YOU HAVE POWER!
YOUR AGENTS

Occasionally, while finishing up your processes, one may encounter the Secret Service. To a "citizen" or a "debtor," this may sound frightening. But as for a creditor, you will look forward to getting your commercial matter resolved by your "agents."

Secret Service. The investigative responsibilities are to detect and arrest persons committing any offense against the laws of the United States relating to coins obligations and securities or the United States and of foreign governments; and to detect and arrest persons violating certain laws relating to the FDIC, Federal land banks, electronic fund transfer frauds, credit and debit card frauds, false identification documents.

Did you know that the duty of the Secret Service is to "detect and arrest persons" that violate the laws pertaining to "securities of foreign governments?" You should know by now that you are a government "foreign" to the US government and all municipalities, and that the credit they enjoy is back by YOUR securities. So, if one of your debtors dishonors your check on a private account where they were supposed to do an "electronic funds transfer," would this constitute a "fraud" on their part? Does this mean that they could be arrested for this? Yes it does! And to aid the Secret Service so that they can investigate the facts and do their duty to you, they must be provided with "information."

Information. An accusation in the nature of an indictment, from which it differs only in being presented by a competent public officer on his oath of office, instead of a grand jury on their oath.

Notary Public. A public officer whose function it is to administer oaths; to attest and certify, by his hand and official seal, certain classes of documents, in order to give them credit and authenticity in foreign jurisdictions; to perform certain official acts, chiefly in commercial matters, such as the protesting of notes and bills, the noting of foreign drafts, and marine protests in cases of loss or damage.

If the debtor has dishonored your acceptance after you have returned it to them and they "argue" the charge still exists, then THEY can now be CHARGED with information or an indictment. To complete this process one must be able to locate a notary public knowledgeable on this subject and willing to do a notarial protest. When the notarial protest process is completed it is as effective as a criminal indictment from a grand jury or a prosecutor. On the civil side it is as effective as a Default Judgment in a State's Superior Court! You should then send an "affidavit of information" along with the completed administrative process to the Secret Service as well as the US Attorney, US Attorney General, US Secretary of Treasury, US Secretary of State, Director of IRS, and your own state's relating officers. This is covered in detail in COURSE 5 – CONTRACTS.

There is another part of the definition of the Secret Service that is important here; Secret Service. The protective responsibilities include protection of … a visiting head of a foreign state or foreign government…unless such protection is decline.

Visiting. In international law, the right of visit or visitation is the right of a cruiser or war-ship to stop a vessel sailing under another flag on the high seas, and send an officer to such vessel to ascertain whether her nationality is what it purports to be. Visitor. A person appointed to visit, inspect, inquire into, and correct irregularities of corporations.

Is there any reason why we would "decline" the offer of someone to protect us and our securities? All the Secret Service is there for is to "ascertain" whether your foreign nationality is what you purport it to be. If you are not sure you are a foreign nation – THEN YOU AREN'T ONE! How then, can one BE a foreign nation? You must think, act and speak like a foreign head.

Usually, the Secret Service will contact you to do an interview with them. When they offer, you should NOT decline as they are there to help you in handling the corporation that dishonored your acceptance. You will be acting as a visitor to "inspect, inquire into and correct irregularities of corporations." To be prepared for this meeting separately package copies of all the administrative process and perfected claims that you have done on each dishonor, then attaching the "affidavit of information" as the cover letter. Now you have everything they need to continue in the "investigation" of the corporation that dishonored you through "electronic transfer fund fraud." Because – that is their job! Now you are acting like a creditor, a principal, a head of a foreign government. A DIPLOMAT!

Be very happy to see them and thank them for looking into this matter for you. Ask them for their card so that you can give them any further information regarding this matter. It would also be impressive to have a card to give to them – this would be very professional and respectful. Encourage them to keep you updated on the progress of the investigation, but let them know that time is of the essence in completing the liquidation of the corporation's equity and that if it was absolutely necessary, you could allow them more time to handle the matter.

If they ask you where does the money come from to pay for the items, you should correct them and say "there is no money, because the UNITED STATES and all municipalities are in bankruptcy and the only currency that exists is the people's credit." You could also tell them "the US Trust Fund is where all of the people's property has been collateralized to create the credit of the nation." If they appear confused, show them a copy of the 73rd Congress, March 9, 1933 where it says;

"(the new money) will be backed by the credit of the nation. It will represent a mortgage on all the homes and property of all the people in the nation."

IN THEIR OWN WRITING THEY AGREE WE ARE THE CREDITORS!

Wow! They would be so impressed and shocked that they had actually witnessed a creditor who knows his business, that they in turn would probably conduct themselves more respectful and business like towards you credit without you knowing that they are charging the "partner," and to keep the "partnership" going without risk of dissolution. Are these guys good or what?

Charge: An encumbrance, lien, or claim; a burden or load; an obligation or duty; a liability; an accusation. A person or thing committed to the care of another. The price of, or rate for, something. Charge account. System of purchasing goods and services on credit, under which customer (you) agrees to settle or make payments on his balance.

No matter what they do to "compel" you into court – DON'T GO. Why would a soveran go to a place and let his servants sort out his affairs for him. Let's say you are handed an arrest warrant by a "peace officer" after you "fail to appear." Look it over and make sure it is correct then say; "I am accepting this charge and am now returning it to you."

Give the warrant back to him as you say it. It does not matter at that point what he does with it as it is a balanced the account, a done deal, finito! Don't take it back, because it has already been discharged. It is a COMPLETED CYCLE OF ACTION. The bailee (officer) then may "escort" you to the "warehouse." The first thing you must do when you get there is ask for your phone call that you are guaranteed to get so that you can call the magistrate that will be able to give you an "appearance bond." You are guaranteed this call even if you have called someone else first. This is the right to go before a magistrate within 24 hours of your "detainment."

When talking to the magistrate make a "statement" as follows; "I want closure on this matter and I do not intend to dispute the facts."

Statement. In a general sense, an allegation; a declaration of matters of fact. A summary of a financial account showing the balance due. Statement of affairs. A balance sheet showing immediate liquidation amounts, usually prepared when bankruptcy is imminent.

When you make a "statement" are you actually asking for the financial account, the balance sheet, so that you can see what the value of the "charge" is? They are in bankruptcy and you are the creditor requesting to see the account of your debtor.

Close/closure. To suspend or stop operations of, to transfer to the main account. [L claudo – to shut, conclude.] Closed account. An account to which no further additions can be made on either side, but which remains still open for adjustment and set-off, which distinguishes it from and account stated.

Set-off. The equitable right to cancel or offset mutual debts or cross demands, commonly used by a bank (you) in reducing a customer's (USA) checking or deposit account in satisfaction of a debt the customer (USA) owes the bank (you).

You see, YOU are the bank! You and your property are the only substance that exists in this fictional system of commerce and you are the only one who can USE it for any purpose. Your substance is the only reason the corporations exist and function at all. The only way to settle the account is to "cancel mutual debt," because being in bankruptcy - THERE IS NO MONEY!

Dispute. A conflict or controversy; an assertion of a right, claim, or demand on one side, met by contrary claims or allegations on the other. The subject of litigation; the matter for which a suit is brought and upon which issue is joined, and in relation to which jurors are called and witnesses examined.

Sounds like DISHONOR to me. So when you say "I do not intend to dispute the facts," what are you saying? I ACCEPT the charges and now I OWN them!

Fact [L facio to do or make] A true statement. A fact is either a state of things that is in existence, or a motion, that is, an event. Evidence. A truth, as distinguished from fiction or error. "Fact" means reality of events or things, the actual occurrence or existence of which is to be determined by evidence.

Admissions. More accurately regarded, they are statements by a party (JOHN), or some one identified with him (John as a partner) in legal interest, of the existence of a fact which is relevant to the cause. As creditor, you are asking to see the statement of account as distinguished from "fiction" which is assumption and presumption. You want to see the basis of the charge – the FACTS.

"I request an appearance bond in order to plead. I request to be released on my own recogniscence until the hearing." So the question you may be asking yourself is "why would I ask for an appearance bond?" To answer this question one must understand the exact definition of this term.

Appear/Appearance. To be in evidence; to be proved. Coming into court by a party to a suit, whether plaintiff or defendant. A special appearance is for the purpose of testing or objecting to the sufficiency of service or the jurisdiction of the court over defendant without submitting to such jurisdiction; Bond. In every case a bond represents debt – its holder is a creditor of the corporation (you) and not a part owner as is the shareholder. The word "bond" is sometimes used more broadly to refer also to unsecured debt instruments.

Does this appearance bond request you to come to court or something else? What name is on the charging instrument entitled COMPLAINT? Your name or the strawman's name? If you say "the strawman," how is he going to make an "appearance?" Just what is the strawman anyway? Can you see a "strawman?" No, but you can show evidence of it. It is an "account" of all the debits the UNITED STATES and municipalities enter to show debt, hence DEBTOR. It is the opposite (public) side of the account which shows the credits (private). And who does the credits belong to? You the "creditor." This being the case, one could see "evidence" of the strawman or the "account which shows the debt."

Does the strawman represent you? No, absolutely not! What then does the strawman represent – who/what created the strawman and is using the credit of the creditor? UNITED STATES OF AMERICA, the plaintiff, who also represents the DEBTOR. Do I hear conflict of interest? So how can this be a judicial proceeding? It is an impossibility. It is a "business transaction in commerce," and the only reason they need you present at the negotiations is so that you, as the principal, can sign for the debtor in order to balance the account. And you say "this is justice?" Maybe it is.

Account. [Old English accompt, from ac – to add + compt – a calculation; from Latin computo – to compute, reckon] Justice. [L justus – just, from jus – to be right, to bind, rights of man] Right. Hebrew yaman - to be right; to be right handed; the right hand or right side; the stronger; the South. Latin regere - to rule. Greek oregein - to stretch out]

Left.　Hebrew semol - wrapping up; properly dark; as
enveloped; the North, the left side, the
idea of cover, assuming the shape of the object beneath.
[Anglo Saxon left – worthless, from lef – weak, infirm.

Do you find it interesting to notice that the debits (debt)
of an account are entered on the "left" side meaning
"worthless" and "assuming the shape" as in the court
assuming you will buy into the game that the name of the
strawman has the same shape as your own? But when you
enter (the court) from the "right" side, it means "the
stronger" and "to rule." It means "substance," "reality." It
means "to make right." Do you think that this is a co-
incidence? I think not.

Hearing. The parties proceeded against or otherwise
involved have right to be heard, in much the same manner as
a trial and such proceedings may terminate a final order.
Audit. Systematic inspection of accounting records involving
analyses, tests, and confirmations. The hearing and
investigation had before and auditor. A formal or official
examination and authentication of accounts, with witnesses,
vouchers, etc. [L audit – he hears, a hearing, from audio – to
hear] Auditor. An officer of the court, assigned to state the
items of debit and credit between the parties in a suit where
accounts are in question, and exhibit the balance. Under
Rules of Civil Procedure in many states, the term "master" is
used to describe those persons formerly known as auditors;

Magistrate. [L magister – a master, from magia – sorcery,
from Greek mageia – the theology of Magicians] Master of
chancery. An officer of a court of chancery who acts as an
assistant to the judge or chancellor. His duties are to inquire
into such matters as may be referred to him by the court,
examine causes, take testimony, take accounts, compute
damages, etc., reporting his findings to the court in such

shape that a decree may be made; RULES OF CIVIL PROCEDURE. 53. Masters (a) Appointment and Compensation. "master" includes a referee, and auditor, an examiner, and an assessor. The master shall not retain the master's report as security for the master's compensation; but when the party ordered to pay the compensation allowed by the court does not pay it after notice and with the time prescribed by the court, the master is entitled to a writ of execution against the delinquent party.

Wow! What officer of the court must state the items of debit and credit and exhibit the balance? You got it, the magistrate holding out "the balance scales of justice." What happens when you are offered the "order to pay" and you do not pay (accept) it? You dishonor, and you will get a writ of execution against you.

(c) Powers.
The master may require the production before the master of evidence upon all matters embraced in the reference, including the production of all books, papers, vouchers, documents, and writings applicable thereto.

(d) (2) Witnesses.
If without adequate excuse a witness fails to appear or give evidence, the witness may be punished as for a contempt and be subjected to the consequences, penalties, and remedies provided in Rules 37 and 45.

(d) (3) Witnesses.
When matters of accounting are in issue before the master, the master may prescribe the form in which the accounts shall be submitted and in any proper case may require or receive in evidence a statement by a certified public accountant who is called as a witness.

(e) Report.
In an action to be tried without a jury, unless otherwise directed by the order of reference, the master shall file with the report a transcript of the proceedings and of the evidence and the original exhibits.

Who is the witness referred to here? It is the accountant or accounting that must provide the court with evidence of the account of the Defendant/ Debtor/Strawman. If they do not provide the court with this evidence, then they are in big trouble!

Account. A detailed statement of the mutual demands in the nature of debit and credit between parties, arising out of contracts or some fiduciary relation. Accountable. Subject to pay; responsible; liable. Accounting/accrual method. A method of keeping accounts which shows expenses incurred and income earned for a given period, although such expenses and income may not have been actually paid or received.

Whatever is debited to the strawman/debtor, we, as a creditor, will show as income. Since there is no money, we can never be paid. So we must take the equity from the corporation or the "service" of the municipality instead as interest payment for using our credit.

In summary, when you ask for the "appearance bond" you are asking to bring evidence into court of the account which shows the debt in order to test the claim without submitting to such jurisdiction so that you can accept the charge and balance the account.

THE GUILTY PLEA

Some of you could be saying "but I don't want to plead GUILTY"! Maybe you don't know what you are saying. Just what does "guilty" mean? Guilty. [Anglo Saxon gildan – to pay, payment] justly chargeable with a crime(commercial liability); Webster's Consolidated Encyclopedic Dictionary 1939 edition.

What are you saying when you say "guilty?" Isn't this a "bad" thing? As you well know, all crimes are commercial liabilities. Instead of saying "I am guilty," you are REALLY saying "I am payment." You are saying "the debtor is chargeable and I, as the creditor am going to pay with my signature as payment, just like all the other credit that I have created with my signature, which the municipalities and corporations have been capitalizing on up to this point. You are saying, "I don't have to get permission from the Federal Reserve System to use MY OWN CREDIT. The Fed intentionally did NOT print enough Federal Reserve Notes to cover the interest payments known as "income taxes" (which creates the national debt), so I am bypassing them and their faulty accounting system and will handle this matter myself as the principal to discharge the national debt."

One must admit that the idea behind this system we are speaking of is absolutely brilliant, if not admirable. Who would have ever thought that the statement "I am guilty" means "I am the creditor who can pay?" There is a universal principle at work here, "what you resist persists," but on the contrary, "what you accept and admire disappears"!

Confession and avoidance. A plea in which one avows and confesses the truth of the averments of fact in the complaint (liability) or declaration, either expressly or by implication, but then proceeds to allege new matter which tends to deprive the facts admitted of their ordinary legal effect, or to obviate, neutralize, or avoid them.

What "new matter" would this be in order to "neutralize" or balance the account? How about requesting that the account evidencing debt be brought into court – the APPEARANCE BOND! What happens when you sign your name on that bond? Bingo! You just created credit, the account is balanced! The debt is now discharged! The charges are dismissed! You see they needed the creditor to give his approval/authority for a block of credit to be produced. That is why you get "court orders." They are really "money orders." Remember, this is simply a commercial transaction. They only want to get your signature to get more credit!

Criminal admissions. A statement by accused, direct or implied, of facts pertinent to issue, and tending, in connection with proof of other facts, to prove his guilt (ability to pay). Confession of Judgment. The act of a debtor in permitting judgment to be entered against him by his creditor, for a stipulated sum, by a written statement to that effect or by warrant of attorney, without the institution of legal proceedings of any kind.

In other words, they are testing you to see if you know that you are the creditor. If you don't know then you aren't one. I just love the two words in the above definition, "issue" as in issue money, and "tending" as in legal tender. This is becoming more and more obvious what the courts are REALLY about. It has nothing to do with justice or the "law" only about ACCOUNTING.

Now what happens when you deny or traverse or argue? You DISHONOR! And at that point, all the rules go out the window. Whatever the "statute" says the fine is valued at no longer matters. Its up to the "magistrate/master/auditor" to make the arbitrary value. NO MERCY!

And what if you "cop a plea to a lesser charge," you just lied! You just DISHONORED! If they try to alter the plea, DON'T BUY IT! It is a trap to get you to dishonor. You want to "accept" the exact charges that they "offered" to you. Once you accept, the contract is yours. Not only that, but the one who makes the charges then gets to pay the bill – not you. This would probably be the Secret Service agent or IRS agent or Prosecutor. Is this country great or what?

What if you do not plead, so the magistrate enters a plea of "NOT GUILTY?" Then he is saying "The man in front of me is not acting like a creditor so he is NOT ABLE TO PAY and thus a debtor." Now they will have to have a trial, as in a "trial balance" to verify the debt.

Try. [French trier – to pick, cull, select, examine; from Latin tritum – to cleanse corn by thrashing; from tra – to pierce] to purify, assay or refine as metals; to test or prove by experiment; to subject to some severe test or experience; to examine or inquire into; a process for testing qualification;

Trial balance. A listing of debit and credit balances of all ledger accounts; all accounts with debit balances are totaled separately from accounts with credit balances. The two totals should be equal.

Jury trial. A body of persons returned from the citizens of a particular district before a court. Return. Something which has had a prior existence will be brought or sent back. Profit on sale, or income from investments. A schedule of information required by governmental bodies, such as the tax return required by the Internal Revenue Service.

Grand jury. Body of citizens, the number of whom varies
from state to state, whose duties consist in determining
whether probable cause exists that a crime (commercial
liability) has been committed and whether an indictment
(true bill) should be returned against one for such a crime.

See, they are still "trying" to get you to accept the charge
so they "return" it to you to give you another chance. It is
part of the administrative procedure to give a second notice.
This is why they have to "try" you with a "trial."

The jury must "find" a person guilty or not guilty so they
can "convict" the defendant.

Find. To discover, to locate, to ascertain and declare.

Finder. In intermediary who contracts to find, introduce, and
bring together parties to a business opportunity, leaving
negotiation and consummation of transaction to the
principals. One who locates a particular type of business
acquisition for a corporation (USA).

Convict. To find (locate) a person (strawman) guilty (liable)
of a criminal (commercial) charge (debt)..

Who would be the intermediary in this matter? The
legislative, judicial and executive systems. They bring some
of the parties together in handcuffs, but they do the job. Now
you, the principal, can negotiate and consume the "business
acquisition" attired in a brilliant orange suit! What a
"business opportunity" of a lifetime!

The main purpose of the trial by jury would be to act in
the capacity of an accountant in order to make a trial balance
and validate the charge or fact on the debit side of the
account of the strawman/debtor to see if it is "accountable."
If they find the debtor "not guilty" or not able to pay and its

creditor does not come forth to sign for the debt, then they throw the collateral in a warehouse for safekeeping. And WHO is the collateral from their viewpoint? When you act like a debtor instead of the creditor, they think YOU are the collateral of the Strawman Corporation.

So the moral of the story is ACCEPT and pay the debt, not DENY and dishonor. Remember, what you resist persists – what you accept and admire disappears. Here is a summary of what you say to the public officials when appropriate;

1. To the officer that hands you a warrant, "I am accepting this charge and am now returning it to you."

2. To the magistrate on the phone, "I want closure on this matter and I do not intend to dispute the facts. I request an appearance bond in order to plead. I request to be released on my own recogniscence until the hearing."

3. To the magistrate at the court room, , "I want closure on this matter and I do not intend to dispute the facts. I request an appearance bond without cost and that you waive the fees on my own personal recogniscence in order to plead." When asked to plead you say, "guilty."

4. When you get the judgment, accept it for value and file it on a UCC-3 as now it becomes your personal property. Now whoever makes the charges (the prosecutor or county attorney, etc.) is the one who has to pay the debt.

YOU WILL BE TRIED

When you go into court to be "tried" in their maritime law of the sea of confusion, you now know the object is to test you to see if you know that you are the creditor. The prosecutor may scoff and mock you in front of the "master" entitled magistrate. They may have been searching for you to get you to come to their negotiation meeting to create worth and value to their claim. Accept and keep your honor. You may be asked questions in order to test you to see how bright you are and how you miraculously discharge debts. But you must keep focused and allow them to prove the basis of the charge. So, hold your position of being the creditor firmly in your mind so you will pass the test.

Below is an interesting analogy of this scenario from II Chronicles 32:31. Read the definitions before reading the verse in order to get a complete grasp of its meaning.

Ambassador. Hebrew luwts – to make mouths at, to scoff, to interpret, make a mock, mocker.

Princes. Hebrew sar – a head person, chief, captain, governor, keeper, master.

Babylon. Heb Babel – confusion; from balal – to overflow, to mix, to feed cattle

Enquire. Heb darash – to tread or frequent, to follow (for pursuit or search), to seek or ask, to worship.   worship. [Anglo Saxon weorthscipe – honor, weorth – worth, value + scipe – shape, make, create]

Wonder. Heb mopheth – conspicuousness, a miracle; from yaphah – to be bright, beautiful.

Land. Heb erets – to be firm, the earth.

Try. Hebrew nacah – to test, to attempt, adventure, assay, prove, tempt, try.

Heart. Heb lebab – the heart (as the most interior), courage, the mind.

II Chronicles 32:31 Howbeit in the business of the ambassadors of the princes of Babylon, who sent unto him to enquire of the wonder that was done in the land, God left him, to try him, that he might know all that was in his heart.

DRILL: Compare the bible verse with the paragraph above it and spot the similarities.

Tried. Greek peirazo – to test, endeavor, scrutinize, entice, discipline, examine, prove; from peira – through the idea of piercing, a test, an experience; from peiro – through, across, cross over to the other side.

Faithful. Greek pistos – trustworthy, trustful, true.

Crown. Greek stephanos – chaplet, wreath as a badge of royalty, a prize in the public games or a symbol of honor.

Revelation 2:10 Fear none of those things which you shall suffer; behold, the devil shall cast some of you into prison, that you may be tried; and you shall have tribulation ten days; be faithful unto death and I will give you a crown of life.

All of our lives we have been told that we are being tested, but did anyone really know what this meant and what to do to pass it? Well, it appears this is a very important test, an opportunity to see if you know who you really are. And if you are true to yourself and continue on regardless of the consequences while playing in the "public games," you will keep your honor and as a soveran, you will receive YOUR crown of life.

October 30, 2014
Paul H O'Neill , Secretary
US Department of the Treasury
1500 Pennsylvania Avenue, NW
Washington, DC 20220

Re: Non-Negotiable Charge Back

Mr. O'Neill:

Enclosed you will find a copy of the Registered Exemption/Contract which I have sent to you to open my Treasury Exemption Account. I accept for value all related endorsements with both UCC 3-419 and HJR-192 of June 5, 1933. Charge my Private Account # 1221101087-0020128095 for the registration fees and command the memory of account number SSN 520-80-1814 to charge the same to the debtor's Order or your Order.

The total amount of this NON-NEGOTIABLE ACCEPTANCE FOR VALUE in the enclosed filing is listed below.

Private Account # 1221101010-0020128095
Pre-paid – Preferred Stock
Priority – Exempt from Levy

_____
Stanley Wade Starr via STANLEY WADE STARR
PO Box 11535
Raleigh, NC 85734

Employer Identification Number: 520801878

Attachments:

1)   Invoice # CRO2219517A, Posted Registered Exemption # RB214518294 for 10,000.00
        2)   Invoice # CRO2219517, Posted Registered Exemption # RB214518285 for an amount
        that has not been assessed by Offeror.
        3)   Copy of UCC-3

Cc: file

Stanley Wade Starr, d.b.a.
Attorney in Fact for
STANLEY WADE STARR, a Trust
PO Box 11535
Freedom, North Carolina 27608

IN THE JUSTICE COURT OF THE STATE OF NORTH CAROLINA

IN AND FOR THE COUNTY OF FREEDOM, PRECINCT
NO._____

STATE OF NORTH CAROLINA)	)
CASE NO. CR02219525	
Plaintiff,)	
	)
Vs.)	
)	
UNCONDITIONAL	
STANLEY WADE STARR, JR.)	
JOSH ALBRITTON,	)
ACCEPTANCE	
HERBERT CRAWFORD,)	
DAVID VIGIL,	)
DIANA L. BOOTH,	)
WHITNEY A. STARR,	)
JUHA KALEVA KIVINEN,	)
	)
Defendants	)
_____)	

Arizona
NOTICE TO AGENT IS NOTICE TO PRINCIPAL   ) ss
NOTICE TO PRINCIPAL IS NOTICE TO AGENT
Pima County   )

1. I, Stanley Wade Starr, d.b.a. Attorney in Fact for STANLEY WADE
STARR, a

Trust, herein "Defendant," hereby state that I am competent to make the following

statements, have knowledge of the facts stated herein, that they are true, correct, complete

and not meant to mislead and are presented in good faith:

      2. On October 30, 2014, Defendant received an offer to contract, entitled FELONY

CRIMINAL COMPLAINT # CR02219525 from SB, d.b.a. Magistrate for FREEDOM COUNTY

JUSTICE COURT. Defendant also received an offer to contract, entitled CRIMINAL

COMPLAINT #CR02219517A, from BG, d.b.a. Deputy Clerk of FREEDOM COUNTY JUSTICE

COURT, herein "Offers."

      3. Defendant does not dispute the facts in this matter. Defendant has

unconditionally accepted and registered the above Offers, and all other parts of the contract

including all documents offered at a future date, pursuant to Power of Acceptance, and

hereby returns them to the Offerors for settlement of the account.

Signed this _____ Day of_____ 2015.

_____

Stanley Wade Starr, d.b.a. Attorney in
Fact for STANLEY WADE STARR, a
Trust

North Carolina   )
) ss

JURAT

Freedom county   )

As a Notary Public for said County and State, I do hereby
certify that on this _____ day of _____
2015 the above mentioned appeared before me and executed
the foregoing. Witness my hand and seal:

_____

Notary Public

Stanley Wade Starr, d.b.a.
Attorney in Fact for
STANLEY WADE STARR, a Trust
PO Box 11535
Freedom, North Carolina 27608

IN THE JUSTICE COURT OF THE STATE OF NORTH CAROLINA

IN AND FOR THE COUNTY OF FREEDOM, PRECINCT
NO._____

STATE OF NORTH CAROLINA	)
	)
CASE NO. CR02219552	
Plaintiff,	)
	)
Vs.	)
	)
APPEARANCE BOND	
STANLEY WADE STARR, JR.	)
JOSH ALBRITTON,	)
HERBERT CRAWFORD,	)
DAVID LONG,	)
DIANA L. BOOTH,	)
WHITNEY A. STARR,	)
JUHA KALEVA KIVINEN,	)
	)
Assigned to:_____	
Defendants	)
_____)	

North Carolina   )
NOTICE TO AGENT IS NOTICE TO PRINCIPAL
) ss
NOTICE TO PRINCIPAL IS NOTICE TO AGENT
Freedom County   )

   I, Stanley Wade Starr, the undersigned principal, hereby enter this
bond for the value of

$10,000.00, and give it to the Clerk of Court for the above noted Case, as recognized by Rule 7.3(b)(1) of FREEDOM Criminal Procedures, so I can be released on my own recognizance and return to this court at the appointed time to plead to the charge(s). I offer to exchange my exemption for the discharge of this bond, for the discharge of the charge(s) against STANLEY WADE STARR, and for the discharge of the principal's body from detention. I request the Court waive all costs, and that the bond be returned to me upon discharge.

I have accepted the charge(s) and return it; therefore, the charge(s) is not controverted. I do not intend to dispute the facts. As the bond is being given, there is no dispute of the facts, and it is apparent that there is no just reason to believe the commission of the offense alleged to have been threatened is imminent, the Defendant shall also be discharged, as is required by ARS 13-3814 and Rule 7.3(b)(1) of North Carolina Criminal Procedures.

I give my word that the Defendant will return to this Court on the _____ day of _____, 2014, at ____: ____ AM PM in room _____ to be present at a hearing before _____ to plead to the charges. Defendant further promises not to commit any criminal offenses and not to depart the state without leave of court prior to the hearing scheduled above. My word is my bond.

This bond is executed by the principal on _____ at
_____.

                                           (Date)

(Place)

_____

Stanley Wade Starr, Principal and Maker

PO Box 11535

Raleigh, North Carolina 27601

IN THE JUSTICE COURT OF THE STATE OF NORTH CAROLINA

IN AND FOR THE COUNTY OF PIMA, PRECINCT NO._____

STATE OF NORTH CAROLINA)
)

      CASE NO.   CR02219517
      Plaintiff,)

      Vs.)

      ORDER OF RELEASE
STANLEY WADE STARR, JR.)
JOSH ALBRITTON,)
HERBERT CRAWFORD,)
DAVID VIGIL,)
DIANA L. BOOTH,)
WHITNEY A. STARR,)
JUHA KALEVA KIVINEN,)
)

Assigned to:_____
         Defendants)
_____)

It is hereby ordered that the Defendant be released on his own recognizance, and to appear in this court and plead to the charge(s) brought in the above noted Case on the _____ day of _____, 2015, at ____ : ____ AM PM in room _____. It is further ordered that Defendant refrain from committing any criminal offenses and that he not depart the state without leave of court.

Dated the _____ day of _____, 2015.

_____

By: _____

Clerk of Court

BEING A SOVERAN

PURPOSE: To bypass public systems and operate privately

•Learn how to establish your own DECLARATION AND TREATY OF PEACE with the world
•Learn how to bypass the court system, and the public recording, registration and taxation systems.
•Learn how to buy property and make it disappear from the public record never to be taxed again
•Learn how to fully organize your private affairs

FINAL PRODUCT: The ability to handle all of your private affairs through your own responsibility.

In the "Consolidated Webster Encyclopedic Dictionary" of 1939, the derivation of sovereign is as follows. [OF soveran, Mod F souveran, from LL superanus, from L super, above, over] the English purposely and erroneously added the "g" in sovereign so that it would include the word "reign"!!! The word was also spelled "soveran" (Miriam Webster's Collegiate Dictionary - Tenth Edition), however the "e" has been erroneously dropped. In the Random House College Dictionary c. 1984, the word has been broken down further, [L super over + -anus -an above].

My conclusion is that the word "sovereign" has been erroneously influenced by the English and the true root definition means "over and above," and that the word should be spelled "soveran", not sovereign and not soveran. So, I am going to make a big leap here and declare that this word is an American word and that we can spell our words the way we want, and use them to communicate whatever we want.

Soveran: over and above, having supreme authority, dominion, rule, rank or power over, beyond jurisdiction, independent and self-governing, autonomous, potent and unlimited in extent. Can a Soveran be under any laws, statutes or "other authority" - or is a Soveran only bound to what one has said, only his own words? However, if a Soveran says that he is under a law or authority - then, of course, he is under the very authority that he spoke of. You may be saying to yourself, "this is too simple, it can't work this easily!" All I have to say to those people is - fine! Have it your way! You can have it however you like. Because - you're the Soveran.

Value: Greek time (tee-may) - a value, money paid, valuables, esteem, dignity itself; from tino - to pay a price (as a penalty), to be punished with. When you value something and you desire it, you are saying, "I do not have the thing that I want so bad and therefore I am punishing myself with it until I get it". What is the product of "TRYING to get something done for a thousand years"? You get a thousand years of TRYING, but you do not get the product do you?

I think that this last commandment is one of the most important rules - You shall not covet. This is where we start remembering how to create again. This is where we take control of our universe and take responsibility for everything we think and say and do. For if we do not guide our own thoughts and our own actions then we will get exactly what we are allowing to be floating around in our minds. If you create "I have" then the physical universe must obey you, and conversely, if you say "I don't have" then the physical universe will also obey you.

How many times have we said "I don't have enough money to pay the bills", or "I have a piece of junk for a car", or "my job sucks"? I just have one question - WHY ARE YOU CREATING THAT? Are you allowing your creation to dictate to you? Are you basing your life on a piece of paper with ink on it (called a bank statement) that you interpret as "you do not have enough money"? All I've got to say is ...Wow, that is an incredible thing that a god can actually create lack! A god can create anything, however you are creating that you DON'T HAVE anything - that is an impossibility. Pat yourself on the back, congratulations - you are actually doing the impossible!!!

I must say that you are doing something incredibly challenging. Wouldn't it be more fun if you decided you wanted something and took responsibility for it from its beginning to its end, that you could imagine you already having it - say a new car. Imagine you seeing your reflection in the shine of the hood, then getting in the car, feeling the cushion of the seat, the aroma of "new car", the steering wheel in your hands, you turning the key, driving away with the wind in you face down a scenic country road, pushing the pedal to the floor for that rush of speed, all the while having a smile on your face. Feels good doesn't it? You have just created a thought that if nourished and embellished upon will result in that dream.

You cannot allow physical barriers to get in the way of your dreams. Matter, energy, space and time are but considerations. Consideration [Latin considero, con together + sidus a star] to fix the mind on; to respect; to take into view or account; to meditate on; to regard; to reflect; important or valuable; making allowance for.

So if you are taking into account, meditating, regarding as important or fixing the mind on a barrier to your dream, then your mind will reflect it into the physical universe and of course, you will get what you make real – your worst fears. It's an honest and true universal principle - crap in/crap out, quality in/quality out.

And what if you do not apply the Ten Commandments to your creation? Deuteronomy 28:68 And the Lord shall bring you into Egypt again with ships, by the way whereof I spoke unto you, You shall see it no more again; and there you shall be sold unto your enemies for bondmen and bondwomen, and no man shall buy you.

What does the Power Elite call UNITED STATES? New Egypt! And it is a fiction – you shall see it no more again. And you have been brought into slavery by way of artificial vessels (ships) called a strawman. And no man bought us as slaves – WE SOLD OURSELVES INTO BONDAGE to our enemies who never paid a dime for us and our credit.

Now you have learned that you do create law every time you think and say a word. You are creating whether you want to or not, it just depends on what you are allowing to be in your mind.

Drill: Go to a mountain or large hill so that you can see a panoramic view of "your world" and read the Ten Commandments out loud one at a time to your creation. Say it like you mean it, like you are talking to the whole universe, repeat the first commandment until you feel it all the way through you, feeling so exhilarated that you just want to explode with emotion and be at one with your universe. Your universe has waited a long time for you to take your throne.

A DECLARATION AND TREATY OF PEACE

Now that you know that you are separate from your creation, you must put it in writing what you want your creation to do. Since you are your own Soveran, you are your own nation and thus you have the responsibility to tell the nations around you what is expected of them.

On July 4, 1776, the forefathers sent to the world a DECLARATION OF INDEPENDENCE stating that united States of America, as a nation, was independent of any rule or authority. This is an incredible statement and the verbiage is awesomely true, however EACH of our forefathers should have sent their own declaration and treaty of peace, not as a nation "jointly," but each as a separate nation - as an independent Soveran.

Since the forefathers did not declare a treaty individually, England conquered the people again, because there was no agreement or treaty between EACH NATION and England. Now for the first time in the history of this planet, each one of you will declare your soveranty to the world with your treaty as the supreme law of the land.

First you must notice the people that are affecting you the most such as the key local, state, national and international officials. They have already published their job descriptions and oaths that they promise to do for you. These actions are called "offers" (offerings) and you as a god and their Creditor must accept them in order to maintain your own honor. If you do not accept them, then you will go into dishonor and YOU will be consumed instead of the offering.

You will be required to read and understand the instructions in order to enact your Treaty as the "Supreme Law of the Land".

INTRODUCTION TO YOUR TREATY

Before we begin your Treaty, it would be beneficial to get some background as to why America is in this present situation. Following is a speech by Representative Traficant who Reports On The Bankruptcy Of The United States,United States Congressional Record, March 1, 1993 VOL. 33, page H-1303 The Speaker - Rep. James Traficant, Jr. (Ohio) addressing the House. Several people have looked in Law Libraries for the above speech and references, however the documents cannot yet be located, therefore this is not verified and cannot be stated as fact. However, Travicant's speech is very eloquent, to the point and can be supported with other documented facts.

Mr. Speaker, we are here now in chapter 11. . . Members of Congress are official trustees presiding over the greatest reorganization of any Bankrupt entity in world history, the U.S. Government. We are setting forth hopefully, a blueprint for our future. There are some who say it is a coroner's report that will lead to our demise.

It is an established fact that the United States Federal Government has been dissolved by the Emergency Banking Act, March 9, 1933, 48 Stat. 1, Public Law 89-719; Declared by President Roosevelt, being bankrupt and insolvent. H. J. R. 192, 73rd. Congress in session June 5, 1933 - Joint Resolution To Suspend The Gold Standard and Abrogate The Gold Clause dissolved the Sovereign Authority of the United States and the official capacities of all United States Government Offices, Officers and Departments and is further evidence that the United States Federal Government exists today in name only.

The receivers of the United States Bankruptcy are the International Bankers, via the United Nations, the World Bank and the International Monetary Fund. All United States Offices, Officials, and Departments are now operating within a defacto status in name only under Emergency War Powers. With the Constitutional Republican form of Government now dissolved, the receivers of the Bankruptcy have adopted a new form of government for the United States. This new form of government is known as a Democracy, being an established Socialist/Communist order under a new governor for America. This act was instituted and established by transferring and/or placing the Office of the Secretary of Treasury to that of the Governor of the International Monetary Fund. Public Law 94-564, page 8, Section H. R. 13955 reads in part: "The U.S. Secretary of Treasury receives no compensation for representing the United States?"

Gold and silver were such a powerful money during the founding of the United States of America, that the founding fathers declared that only gold and silver coins can be "money" in America. Since gold and silver coinage were heavy and inconvenient for a lot of transactions, they were stored in banks and a claim check was issued as a money substitute. People traded their coupons as money, or "currency." Currency is not money, but a money substitute. Redeemable currency must promise to pay a dollar equivalent in gold or silver money. Federal Reserve Notes (FRN's) made no such promises, and are not "money." A Federal Reserve Note is a debt obligation of the federal United States government, not "money." The federal United States government and the U.S. Congress were not and have never been authorized by the Constitution for the United States of America to issue currency of any kind, but only lawful money, - gold and silver coin.

It is essential that we comprehend the distinction between real money, and paper money substitute. One cannot get rich by accumulating money substitutes, one can only get deeper in debt. We the People no longer have any "money." Most Americans have not been paid any "money" for a very long time, perhaps not in their entire life. Now do you comprehend why you feel broke? Now, do you understand why you are "bankrupt," along with the rest of the country?

Federal Reserve Notes (FRN's) are unsigned checks written on a closed account. FRN's are an inflatable paper system designed to create debt through inflation (devaluation of currency). Whenever there is an increase of the supply of a money substitute in the economy without a corresponding increase in the gold and silver backing, inflation occurs.

Inflation is an invisible form of taxation that irresponsible governments inflict on their citizens. The Federal Reserve Bank who controls the supply and movement of FRN's has everybody fooled. They have access to an unlimited supply of FRN's, paying only for the printing costs of what they need. FRN's are nothing more than promissory notes for U.S. Treasury securities (T-Bills) - a promise to pay the debt to the Federal Reserve Bank.

There is a fundamental difference between "paying" and "discharging" a debt. To pay a debt, you must pay with value or substance (i.e. gold, silver, barter or a commodity). With FRN's, you can only discharge a debt. You cannot pay a debt with a debt currency system. You cannot service a debt with a currency that has no backing in value or substance. No contract in common law is valid unless it involves an exchange of "good and valuable consideration." Unpayable debt transfers power and control to the sovereign power structure that has no interest in money, law, equity or justice because they have so much wealth already. Their lust is for power and control. Since the inception of central banking, they have controlled the fates of nations.

The Federal Reserve System, is based on the Canon law and the principles of sovereignty protected in the Constitution and the Bill of Rights. In fact, the international bankers used a "Canon Law Trust" as their model, adding stock and naming it a "Joint Stock Trust." The U.S. Congress had passed a law making it illegal for any legal "person" to duplicate a "Joint Stock Trust" in 1873. The Federal Reserve Act was legislated post-facto (1870), although post-facto laws are strictly forbidden by the Constitution. (1:9:3)

The Federal Reserve System is a sovereign power structure separate and distinct from the federal United States government. The Federal Reserve is a maritime lender, and/or maritime insurance underwriter to the federal United States operating exclusively under Admiralty/Maritime law. The lender underwriter bears the risks, and the Maritime law compelling specific performance in paying the interest, or premiums are the same.

Assets of the debtor can also be hypothecated (to pledge something as a security without taking possession of it) as security by the lender or underwriter. The Federal Reserve Act stipulated that the interest on the debt was to be paid in gold. There was no stipulation in the Federal Reserve Act for ever paying the principal.

Prior to 1913, most Americans owned clear, allodial title to property, free and clear of any liens or mortgages until Federal Reserve Act (1913). "Hypothecated" all property within the federal United States to the Board of Governors of the Federal Reserve, - in which the Trustees (stockholders) held legal title, the U.S. citizen (tenant, franchisee) was registered as a "beneficiary" of the trust via his/her birth certificate. In 1933, the federal United States hypothecated all of the present and future properties, assets and labor of their "subjects," the 14th. Amendment U.S. citizens, to the Federal Reserve System.

In return, the Federal Reserve System agreed to extend the federal United States corporation all the credit "money substitute" it needed. Like any other debtor, the federal United States government had to assign collateral and security to their creditors as condition of the loan. Since the federal United States didn't have any assets, they assigned the private property of their "economic slaves," the U.S. citizens, as collateral against the unpayable federal debt. They also pledge the unincorporated federal territories, national parks forest, birth certificates, and nonprofit organizations, as collateral against the federal debt. All has already been transferred as payment to the international bankers.

Unwittingly, America has returned to its pre-American Revolution, Feudal roots whereby all land is held by a sovereign and the common people had no rights to hold allodial title to property. Once again, we the People are the tenants and sharecroppers renting our own property from a Sovereign in the guise of the Federal Reserve Bank. We the People have exchanged one master for another.

This has been going on for over eighty years without the "informed" knowledge: Of the American people, without a voice protesting loud enough. Now it's easy to grasp why America is fundamentally bankrupt.

Why don't more people own their properties outright? Why are 90% of Americans mortgaged to the hilt and have little or no assets after all debts and liabilities have been paid? Why does it feel like you are working harder and harder and getting less and less?

We are reaping what has been sown, and the result of our harvest is a painful bankruptcy, and a foreclosure on American property, precious liberties, and a way of life. Few of our elected representatives in Washington, D.C. have dared to tell the truth. The federal United States is bankrupt. Our children will inherit this unpayable debt, and the tyranny to enforce paying it.

America has become completely bankrupt in world leadership, financial credit and its reputation for courage, vision and human rights. This is an undeclared economic war. Bankruptcy, and economic slavery of the most corrupt order! Wake up America! Take back your country.

INSTRUCTIONS FOR ENACTING YOUR TREATY AS LAW

PURPOSE: As a Creditor of UNITED STATES and all other sub-corporations private and public, you are owed equity and interest for the gold and all property that you "loaned" them starting March 9, 1933 to date. There is NO MONEY. In order to start getting your equity back, you must NOTICE your DEBTORS of what you expect them to do and the consequences if they do not comply, but first you must ESTABLISH THE LAW. Your treaty is a contract to the WHOLE WORLD and tells the world what you want and how things are going to be done in this CREDITOR/DEBTOR relationship. This file contains all the documents you will need to PERFECT YOUR TREATY and TAKE BACK YOUR EQUITY;

A. Instructions
B. Treaty
C. .Notice of Default and Entry of Assent to Contract
D. Certificate of Assent - from a third party witness saying no response was received
E. Acceptance to Contract - to be filed with Secretary of State.

1. The following steps are sequence of events that must occur to get your treaty established and enacted as the supreme law of the land.
   a. Word process the Treaty for all of the correct information
   b. Print the Treaty out, read it several times for correctness and

MAKE SURE YOU DESIGNATE A THIRD PARTY RECEIVER WITH NAME AND ADDRESS, then get it notarized
   c. Send the Treaty by registered mail, return receipt so you have proof that they received your Contract you are in the process of creating.
   d. If you have not received a response in twenty (20) days, send Notice of Default and Entry of Assent to Contract allowing Respondents ten (10) additional days to respond.
   e. Send the copies of the above documents to the Respondent(s) and keep the originals
   f. After ten (10) additional days get take the Certificate of Assent to the THIRD PARTY RECEIVER and have them Notarize their signature.
   g. Word process the ACCEPTANCE TO CONTRACT and notarize it
   h. Take all of the Notices that you have done from the Treaty and arrange them in a package from the first on the bottom to the Certificate of Assent on the top.

i. Place the ACCEPTANCE TO CONTRACT on top of the package, copy the package, and file a UCC-3 Addendum onto your original UCC-1 with SECRETARY OF STATE for your state.

2. You now have a perfected claim.

THIS IS A WORK IN PROGRESS. IT IS CERTAIN THAT THERE WILL BE IMPROVEMENTS TO THIS PROCESS AND WE WILL STRIVE TO GET THE INFORMATION TO YOU. IN THE MEANTIME, LEARN IT, IMPROVE ON IT YOURSELF, AND SPREAD IT TO EVERYONE YOU KNOW WHO IS DETERMINED TO BE RESPONSIBLE FOR THE CREATION OF THEIR WORLD.

John Henry Doe

A Declaration and Treaty of Peace to the World
North Carolina   )
NOTICE TO AGENT IS NOTICE TO PRINCIPAL

) ss

NOTICE TO PRINCIPAL IS NOTICE TO AGENT
Freedom County   )

Treaty # 00701-JHD

ARTICLE I
Parties, Capacity and Definitions

1. Sovereign. I exist as a sovereign being. My authority for this contract is the age-old, timeless, and universal respect for the intrinsic power, property, and responsibilities of the sovereign being. I choose to comply with the principles of mutual respect which serve to bring harmony to society. I have sovereign immunity and therefore, my power to contract and enforce contracts is unlimited unless I infringe on the rights of others.

2. Sovereign Nation. I operate through a genetic entity, named John Henry Doe, made in my own image, which I give life and power to. I act in the capacity of a foreign nation without subjects who rules autonomously and am not subject to any entity or jurisdiction anywhere. I am a Creditor, hereinafter "Creditor", of the Respondents listed below and am exempt from levy from any entity.

3. Sovereign Person. I use an artificial entity called a trust, entitled JOHN HENRY DOE, an image of John Henry Doe, to conduct commercial business and to interface with other legal fictions in regard to contracts, transactions, negotiations and judgments. Respondents - Persons: are artificial entities created by spiritual beings for the purpose of participating in commerce.

4. The following are legal persons and artificial entities called private corporations: UNITED NATIONS and its sub-corporations, UNITED STATES and its sub-corporations including the STATE OF ARIZONA and the other 49 STATES and all their COUNTIES, MUNICIPALITIES and

other sub-corporations, INTERNATIONAL MONETARY FUND, FEDERAL RESERVE BANK and all other registered corporations on planet earth.

Respondents - Natural Persons: Spiritual beings who have agreed to relinquish their power and authority and to an artificial entity of their own creation which they now must obey.

The following natural persons are public citizens, contracted under private corporate policy and employed as agents for the principals of their respective private corporations: Paul O'Neill, d.b.a. Secretary of Treasury of the United States, d.b.a. Governor for the International Monetary Fund, d.b.a. Governor of the Federal Reserve Bank, Charles O. Rosotti, Internal Revenue Service, IRS, Kofi Annan, d.b.a. Secretary General of the United Nations, George W. Bush, d.b.a. President of the United States, Norman Minetta, d.b.a. Secretary of Transportation of the United States, Colin Powell, d.b.a. US Secretary of State, Tom Ridge, d.b.a. Director of Homeland Security United States, Jane Hull, d.b.a. Governor of the State of Arizona, Betsy Bayless, d.b.a. Secretary of State of the State of Arizona, Janet Napolitano, d.b.a. Attorney General of the State of Arizona, and all agents thereof.

ARTICLE II
History

1. Suspension of the Government of the united States of America. On December 20, 1860, the congressmen of the southern States of America walked out of congress in session because they did not agree with the policies the northern States had forced on them. This action caused a State of Emergency which suspended the Republic of the united States of America and therefore suspended the constitution and its government. Over 140 years since that time America has been without a government, however, through contract the republic was replaced by a foreign operated private corporation called UNITED STATES.

2. Invasion of America. On February 21, 1871, an elite group of private bankers created a private corporation in England, entitled DISTRICT OF COLUMBIA and copyrighted the name UNITED STATES, hereinafter "US." The goal of the foreign corporation being, to invade America and gradually change its policies to better control the commerce of the land. The US,

subtly and efficiently, replaced the republic called united States of America in its functions and duties. In the beginning the jurisdiction of the US extended only to the ten miles square of the area of Washington D.C. plus the territories that the US had purchased, however the US eventually took control of the 50 State republics by creating a corporation for each State named "STATE OF..." plus the corresponding State's name.

3.Attack on America. On October 6, 1917, the UNITED STATES passed a corporate policy called the Trading with the Enemy Act. In Section 2, sub-section (c) of the Act it defines the enemy as "other than the citizens of the United States". The American people were sovereign which makes them "foreign governments" to the UNITED STATES and therefore, the sovereigns unknowingly became enemies of the State. On March 3, 1933, the Trading with the Enemy Act was then amended in order to confiscate gold from the US citizens (not the American Sovereigns) who were reimbursed with "emergency money", issued by a private corporation known as the Federal Reserve Bank, which represented debt owed to the Federal Reserve Bank. A dollar of gold was exchanged for a dollar of debt owed to the Federal Reserve Bank plus interest (Income Tax). Basically all Americans lost two dollars in the exchange.

4. History of Current Contract. On March 9, 1933, due to impending bankruptcy, the UNITED STATES made a "New Deal" with the US citizens (not the American Sovereigns) entitled, Senate Document No. 43, 73rd Congress, 1st Session, herein "contract". The contract stated, "It (Federal Reserve Notes, Bills and Bonds, etc.) will represent a mortgage on all the homes and other property of all the people in the Nation." As a result, title of all property was turned over to the State as evidenced by the statement in the contract, "The ownership of all property is in the State". In order to account for the monetary increases gained by the use of the people's property and production, the UNITED STATES created artificial entities termed "Persons," for each of the people using the people's own names, however spelled in all capital letters. For example, John Doe the man would have a Person entitled JOHN DOE named after him.

5. Offer and Acceptance of Contract. In 1933, the private foreign operated corporation called UNITED STATES made an

offer to contract with my great grandfather, an American Sovereign, hereinafter "Principal". The US was in heavy debt to the Federal Reserve Bank so the US passed a law that required all US citizens to turn in their gold. The Principal, being sovereign, did not have to comply with this private corporate policy, however he wanted to help the US get out of debt, so he accepted the offer to contract and loaned the US his gold, property and production for the remainder of his life. The contract has continued through the life of my grandfather, my father and now with me for a total of 68 years with the UNITED STATES acting as fiduciary heir and thereby receiving the benefit of my family's property, production and exemption pursuant to the contract.

6. Discharge of Public Debt. On June 5, 1933, part of the contract, entitled House Joint Resolution 192, stipulated that since the UNITED STATES removed the gold and substance required to "pay" off debt, they then had to state that "any obligation which purports to give the obligee the right to require payment....in an amount in money of the UNITED STATES measured thereby, is declared to be against public policy." This essentially was an insurance policy that protected legislators from conviction for fraud and treason against the American people for taking away their property. It also protected the American people from damages caused by this unconventional action of the UNITED STATES.

7. Increasing the National Debt. Since the U.S. Secretary of Treasury was the delegated Trustee of the bankruptcy, it was his duty to discharge all public debt that the creditor of the bankruptcy would be charged with (pursuant to the copyrighted U.S. Rules of Bankruptcy). As creditors, the Principal and his successor heirs should have accepted every charge of debt they were offered, by the Respondents, then sign and remit the discharge to the Trustee for settlement of their account with the corporate US as the debtor. However, the Principals as creditors mistakenly have been attempting to pay debts with debt instruments, entitled Federal Reserve Notes, inadvertently DOUBLING the debt instead of CANCELING it, thus increasing the national debt.

8. Creation of Person. On or about January 22, 1958, The UNITED STATES under contract with the creditor of the bankruptcy, and through my existence and authority, created an

artificial entity called a trust entitled JOHN HENRY DOE, hereinafter "Person". The application for the birth certificate for that Person, herein "title", created by the state when John Henry Doe was born, was the instrument through which the Person was created. The title was then registered in the commercial registry through a constructive contract created by the State.

9. Acknowledgement to Fiduciary Heir. Since the contract of March 9, 1933, the fiduciary heirs have skillfully turned the insolvent UNITED STATES corporation and its sub-corporations into solvent entities, as evidenced by the Comprehensive Annual Financial Reports and combined budget reports showing assets in excess of 70 trillion US dollars, Repository Trust accounts in excess of 30 trillion dollars, and large denomination repurchase agreements (redemption accounts) in M3 money. This is an incredible accomplishment and the fiduciary heir and their agents are thanked for their service and are highly commended for this great achievement.

ARTICLE III
Declarations and Claims

1. Secured Claim. In June 2000, I, John Henry Doe, filed a UCC-1 Financing Statement which included the Security Agreement between the trust, entitled JOHN HENRY DOE, as the DEBTOR, and John Henry Doe, the superior claimant of right as Creditor. This act secured title to the Person created by the state and secures to John Henry Doe all property attached to the Person under the title of JOHN HENRY DOE. This claim is undisputed and therefore stands by fiat that John Henry Doe, hereinafter "Creditor", is Holder In Due Course and creditor of record of JOHN HENRY DOE.

2. Redemption. I hereby claim my exemption and inheritance of right from my fiduciary heir, within the UNITED STATES corporation and initially claim $100,000,000.00 (One Hundred Million Dollars) to be returned to me by the fiduciary heir over an undetermined period of time at my discretion. This claim acts as the reacquisition of the security that the Principal issued and now I, as his heir, hereby accept pursuant to the terms of this provision.

3. Sovereign Immunity. All corporate, state, national and international "constitutions, laws, statutes, ordinances, regulations, rules, codes, orders, proclamations, corporate policy and public

policy" are private copyrighted material. I do not possess a license nor have authority to use such copyrighted material, and conversely, such material or any other material or entity has no authority over Creditor's property or personal affairs and is herein accepted for value whenever Respondents attempt to enforce it on Creditor. Creditor will consider the above private corporate policy when dealing with U.S. and other national citizens for the purpose of maintaining harmony in society. Creditor's immunity as a sovereign is absolute, and the terms and conditions of this contract are enforceable and stand regardless of any condition in the future including State of Emergency, Martial Law, Declaration of War and all other conditions.

4. In Itinere Status: I hereby declare my in itinere status as a foreign sovereign according to the principles of law as stated by the Hague Convention of October 5, 1961 and the Vienna Convention of April 18, 1961 witnessed by the seal from the Secretary of State of West Virginia #0564646.

5. Acceptance of Contracts. All contracts i.e., adhesion, constructive, gratuitous, onerous, quasi, and other applications for license, permits, general benefits, and specific benefits listed assumed or presumed in the Individual Master File maintained by the Internal Revenue Service, IRS or any other agency or quasi agency of the UNITED STATES and United Nations, and all other invisible contracts have NOT been made with the Creditor, but with the Person created by the state. I, as John Henry Doe, hereby accept for value all public contracts, presentments and other agreements with a qualified acceptance each and every time a public employee or officer of any rank presents an offer to contract with the Person or with the Creditor as the presumed surety for the Person, from this day forward.

6. Foreign Currency. The Respondents have been using the credit of the Creditor up to this point in time as security for Federal Reserve Notes, Treasury Bills, Notes and Bonds. From this point forward, Creditor, as a foreign nation, has full authority to authorize use of his own credit for discharge of public debts by using any instrument of choice that serves to sufficiently communicate such transaction intent to the party receiving said credit, and acts as a private contract between the parties, thereby excluding any and all third party entities which include the UNITED STATES, FEDERAL RESERVE BANK, INTERNATIONAL MONETARY FUND and all agents thereof that may attempt to impede commerce of Creditor. I hereby

accept the responsibility for increasing the national debt of the UNITED STATES and will henceforth correct the inappropriate actions made by the Principal, his successor heirs, and myself by accepting and remitting any further debt obligations for settlement and setoff to the particular Respondent making the offer as an agent of the US Secretary of Treasury.

7. Unlimited Liability. Consistent with the eternal principle of ultimate acceptance, Creditor hereby accepts full responsibility for creating everything in his world, constructive and destructive, and if another's rights are violated, Creditor alone will put the injured party back to a position as good as they were before the incident.

8. Copyright and Licensing. Notice is hereby given that the names John Henry Doe and JOHN HENRY DOE, and all of the laws issued in this private treaty are copyrighted property, and Respondents must have permission from Creditor to use this material by obtaining a copyright license from Creditor. Necessary licensing includes the use of Creditor's names for the purposes of exemption, deduction, and as security for printing Federal Reserve Notes and all other instruments. Since all Respondents are foreign corporations and agents to the land called America, they are also required to obtain a business license from Creditor to operate in commerce.

9. Notice of Non-consent. Notice is hereby given that Creditor, as a foreign nation, does not consent to Respondents, as persons and private corporations, judging him on any matter in any instance, at any location, at any time now or in the future. Creditor does not subordinate his position of record as Creditor over the Respondents as Debtors.

10. Declaration of Peace. In October of 2001, the U.S. Senate and House passed a Public Policy called "The Uniting and Strengthening of America Act". I hereby accept this act as an offer of peace from the UNITED STATES and Respondents to the American Sovereigns and myself with a qualified acceptance that it is to be used to defend American Sovereigns from terrorism foreign and domestic.

ARTICLE IV
Delegation of Duties

1. Delegation of Fiduciary Duty. Unless otherwise expressed by Creditor, the Arizona Secretary of State, Betsey Bayless, and

successor office holders, are hereby delegated as the Fiduciary of the trust known as JOHN HENRY DOE. Pursuant to the 1933 contract, "The ownership of all property is in the State; individual so-called ownership is only by virtue of Government, i.e., law amounting to mere user". Since the State has claimed ownership of all property, the Delegated Fiduciary will henceforth be responsible for the property that is held for the Creditor. Responsibilities include the paying of all property taxes for land and personal property, paying for maintenance, insurance, permits, licensing and registration fees for vehicles and all property, and the payment of all fines for civil and criminal charges the Person or Creditor may be charged with. Creditor will use the property as "mere user" for any and every purpose of his choice, for an unlimited period of time without hindrance from any entity.

2. Delegation of Surety Duty. Creditor hereby delegates the U.S. Secretary of Treasury, Paul O'Neill, and successor office holders, as the Surety of the exempt private trust known as JOHN HENRY DOE and the property, repository accounts and accruing annuity therein claimed by the Creditor. The Surety will perform monetary transfers whenever requested by the Creditor and will honor any instrument that the Creditor wishes to use as long as it communicates the appropriate information to do the transaction for discharge of all debt public and private. As officer over the Internal Revenue Service, IRS, the Surety is also charged with the duty of collecting taxes for Creditor from the Respondents as Debtors.

3. Delegation of Security Duty. Creditor hereby delegates the U.S. Director of Homeland Security, Tom Ridge and successor office holders, as the officer in charge and the U.S. Secret Service for defending the Creditor as a visiting head of a foreign government, and to protect all the possessions and property of the Creditor as well as the Person against all acts of terrorism foreign and domestic. Investigative responsibilities of the U.S. Secret Service are to detect and arrest persons committing any offense against the laws of this treaty relating to drafts, obligations, and securities of the Creditor as a foreign government.

4. Delegation of Peace Keeping Duty. Creditor hereby delegates Kofi Annan, d.b.a. Secretary General of the United Nations and successor office holders, as the officer in charge of preventing war, providing justice by the principles of Tacit Law, and promoting welfare and human rights of all peoples.

5. Delegation of Power of Attorney. Creditor hereby delegates John Ashcroft, d.b.a. Attorney General of United States, and Janet Napolitano, d.b.a. Attorney General of the State of Arizona and successor office holders, as the chief law officers of the Creditor, being created by contracts, whose office is to represent the trust, entitled JOHN HENRY DOE, exhibit information, and prosecute for the Creditor in matters criminal, and to file bills in the Treasury in any matter concerning the Creditor's revenue.

ARTICLE V
Terms and Conditions

1. Oath of Office. An Oath of Office must be taken by each of the above named Respondents - Natural Persons to uphold this contract and the agreements therein to the best of their ability and must swear to protect and serve it from enemies foreign and domestic. Assent to this contract is deemed that the Respondents have taken the oath.

2. Violations and Sanctions. Herein are the penalties for violations of the contract that Respondents and their agents have assented to and agree to compensate Creditor for in the event a violation occurs;

A. $10,000,000.00 (Ten Million Dollars) per person involved for each instance of arrest and incarceration conducted by Respondents or their agents and the same amount each day thereafter until released;
B. $1,000,000.00 (One Million Dollars) per person for each instance of impeding Creditor's commerce in anyway whatsoever or triple damages, whatever is greater;
C. $1,000,000.00 (One Million Dollars) per person for each instance of arrest, search and seizure, damage of Creditor's property, court order, warrant, or charge issued by Respondents;
D. $1,000,000.00 (One Million Dollars) per person for each instance of harassment, threat or any act of terrorism or war from any one of the Respondents or their agents.
E. $1,000,000.00 (One Million Dollars) per person for each instance of unauthorized deduction against Creditor's tax exempt status.

1.Arbitration of violations. All violations of this contract will be settled through private administrative process by both parties involved. In the event the offender(s) assent to all charges, a panel of three (3) disinterested parties under the determination of an International Tribune, will act as the judicial process to issue final judgment according the principles of Tacit Law. The judgment will then be recorded and perfected as a claim and executed under involuntary bankruptcy in the offender's private capacity. The judgment will also act as a confession by the offenders, and the Attorney General of the state in which the violation occurred will be notified of the decision so that Respondents shall prosecute the offenders criminally as required by the applicable copyrighted corporate policy that Respondents have sworn to uphold.

2. Caveat. In the absence of a clear written contract between us, my affidavit will result in a clear understanding and meeting of the minds of the parties clearly identified. Your failure to properly and timely respond is your agreement with the statements and averments I have made herein. This affidavit stands as truth in commerce unless properly rebutted within twenty-one (21) days of your receipt of this affidavit. Your response must be made by affidavit with a notarized signature, rebutting my affidavit point by point with documentation to support your statements, and must note it is "true, correct, and complete, and not meant to mislead," and forward an original to the Notary Public, as a third party public official witness, c/o Diana L. Booth, 6942 W. Walking M, Tucson, AZ 85746.

It has been said, so it is done.

Signed and Sealed this _____ day of _____ 2015.

_____

John Henry Doe
North Carolina   )
) ss
ACKNOWLEDGEMENT
Freedom County)

As a Notary Public for said County and State, I do hereby certify that on
this _____ day of _____
2015 the above mentioned appeared before me and executed the
foregoing. Witness my hand and seal:

_____Notary Public

Copies forwarded to the following:

Kofi Annan
        Paul O'Neill
UN Secretary General
        US Secretary of Treasury
UNITED NATIONS BUILDING RM S-378
        DEPARTMENT OF TREASURY
New York, NY 10017   1500
Pennsylvania Ave NW

        Washington D.C. 20220

Charles O. Rossotti
        Barack Obama
Internal Revenue Service, IRS   President
of the UNITED STATES
1111 Constitution Ave NW
        1600 Pennsylvania Avenue
Washington, DC 20224-0002
        Washington DC 20500

Norman Minetta   Tom
Ridge
US Secretary of Transportation   Director
of Homeland Security
400 Seventh Street, SW   1600
Pennsylvania Avenue
Washington, DC 20590
        Washington DC 20500

Jane Hull
 Betsey Bayless
Governor of the State of Arizona   Arizona
Secretary of State
Arizona Executive Office of the Governor   1700 W.
Washington Street
1700 W. Washington Ave.   Phoenix,
Arizona 85007
Phoenix, Arizona 85007

Janet Napolitano   Colin L.
Powell
Office of Attorney General
 Secretary of State
Department of Law
 U.S. Department of State
1275 W. Washington Street
Phoenix, Arizona 85007
 Washington, D.C.

 20520-6810

John Henry Doe

A Declaration and Treaty of Peace to the World

Respondents: Paul O'Neill, d.b.a. Secretary of Treasury of the United States, d.b.a. Governor for the International Monetary Fund, d.b.a. Governor of the Federal Reserve Bank, Charles O. Rossotti, Internal Revenue Service, IRS, Kofi Annan, d.b.a. Secretary General of the United Nations, George W. Bush, d.b.a. President of the United States, Norman Minetta, d.b.a. Secretary of Transportation of the United States, Tom Ridge, d.b.a. Director of Homeland Security United States, Jane Hull, d.b.a. Governor of the State of Arizona, Betsy Bayless, d.b.a. Secretary of State of the State of Arizona, Janet Napolitano, d.b.a. Attorney General of the State of Arizona, and all agents thereof.

NOTICE OF DEFAULT AND ENTRY OF ASSENT TO CONTRACT

Contract # 100701-JHD

North Carolina   )
NOTICE TO AGENT IS NOTICE TO PRINCIPAL

) ss

NOTICE TO PRINCIPAL IS NOTICE TO AGENT
Freedom County   )

    Notice is hereby given, that the above named respondents are in Default upon the contract, entitled Declaration and Treaty of Peace # 100701-JHD dated September 22, 2001, and therefore an Assent to Contract has been entered upon them.

    By the terms and conditions of the agreement contained in the Creditor's affidavit, you were under obligation to timely and in good faith protest and make proper presentment with proof of your claim or interest. Your failure to do so is a dishonor and places you in agreement with the terms and conditions of the contract.

    By your default, you are deemed to be under the new terms and conditions of our original contract and have therefore waived all of your rights to your original presentment and terms. Any attempt to collect on your original presentment places you personally at risk for any damages incurred per this contract and may subject you to criminal sanctions and involuntary bankruptcy.

You are given ten (10) additional days for an opportunity to cure by responding to the contract before PERFECTION OF THE CONTRACT is made by sending an original affidavit to the specified Notary Public as a third party public official witness.

_____ Date

John Henry Doe

North Carolina   )
) ss

ACKNOWLEDGEMENT

Freedom County   )

As a Notary Public for said County and State, I do hereby certify that on this _____ day of _____
2015 the above mentioned appeared before me and executed the foregoing. Witness my hand and seal:

_____

Notary Public

CERTIFICATE OF ASSENT

North Carolina)
) ss
Freedom County)

I, Diana L. Boone, am the notary to whom all communications are to be mailed regarding the contract entitled John Henry Doe, Declaration and Treaty of Peace, Treaty # 100701-JHD, herein "contract".

Pursuant to Arizona Revised Statutes 47-3505(b), and Uniform Commercial Code 3-505(b), Notice of Protest is hereby given with Certificate of Dishonor regarding the following:

On July 16, 2015, I notarized a Declaration and Treaty of Peace from John Henry Doe, herein "Affiant", to the following Respondents who were given 10 days to respond.

Paul O'Neill, d.b.a. Secretary of Treasury of the United States, d.b.a. Governor for the International Monetary Fund, d.b.a. Governor of the Federal Reserve Bank, Charles O. Rosotti, Internal Revenue Service, IRS, Kofi Annan, d.b.a. Secretary General of the United Nations, George W. Bush, d.b.a. President of the United States, Norman Minetta, d.b.a. Secretary of Transportation of the United States, Tom Ridge, d.b.a. Director of Homeland Security United States, Jane Hull, d.b.a. Governor of the State of Arizona, Betsy Bayless, d.b.a. Secretary of State of the

State of Arizona, Janet Napolitano, d.b.a. Attorney General of the State of Arizona, and all agents thereof.

As of this date, no response had been delivered to me, the designated receiver. I interviewed John Henry Doe, whose affidavit is attached to this Notarial Protest. John Henry Doe has stated to me by affidavit that Petitioner has received no response to said Contract at any other mailing location. Based on the foregoing information, Respondent has dishonored John Henry Doe's contract by non-acceptance and/or non-performance and have therefore assented to the terms and conditions in said Contract.

_____

Party Witness

Diana L. Booth, Third

(Stamp)   (Seal)

John Henry Doe
A Declaration and Treaty of Peace to the World

ACCEPTANCE OF CONTRACT

Treaty # 100701-JHD

North Carolina   )   NOTICE TO AGENT IS NOTICE TO
PRINCIPAL
) ss   NOTICE TO PRINCIPAL IS NOTICE TO AGENT
Freedom County)

I, John Henry Doe, herein "Creditor", state the facts contained herein are true, correct, complete, and not misleading, to the best of my personal knowledge.

This is timely notice that I except for value the attached binding contract, entitled A Declaration and Treaty of Peace to the World # 100701-JHD; and CERTIFICATE OF ASSENT, from a third party Public Official as Notary Public; and the assent of the following natural persons to Creditor's contract:

Paul O'Neill, d.b.a. Secretary of Treasury of the United States, d.b.a. Governor for the International Monetary Fund, d.b.a. Governor of the Federal Reserve Bank, Charles O. Rossotti, Internal Revenue Service, IRS, Kofi Annan, d.b.a. Secretary General of the United Nations, George W. Bush, d.b.a. President of the United States, Norman Minetta, d.b.a. Secretary of Transportation of the United States, Colin L. Powell, d.b.a. Secretary of State United State, Tom Ridge, d.b.a. Director of Homeland Security United States, Jane Hull, d.b.a. Governor of the State of Arizona, Betsy Bayless, d.b.a. Secretary of State of the State of Arizona, Janet Napolitano, d.b.a. Attorney General of the State of Arizona, and all agents thereof.

This is notice that this Treaty is creditor's property exempt from levy.

It has been said, so it is done.   Signed and Sealed this
_____ day of _____ 2015.

_____

John Henry Doe
North Carolina   )
) ss
ACKNOWLEDGEMENT
Freedom County   )

As a Notary Public for said County and State, I do hereby certify that on this _____ day of_____ 2015, the above mentioned appeared before me and executed the foregoing. Witness my hand and seal:

_____

Notary Public

INTERFERENCE BY THIRD PARTY
HOW TO MAKE THEM DISAPPEAR

Purpose: To prevent the interference and trespass of a third party into your private contract.

In your commercial activities, you may be met by a third party who wishes to interfere with your private affairs. You must keep focused on the completion of every contract without being distracted by any outside influence such as an attorney.

Someone at a bank may have dishonored your instrument at one point so you followed through with your private remedy and created a contract with the one who dishonored you. It is very important to have the name of the one who signed the instrument evidencing dishonor. You cannot make a private contract with a bank or other fictitious entity (corporation) in the private side, because you cannot see a fiction. You can only contract with a man or a woman that has signed a letter or other document, but you cannot contract with a fictitious entity.

If you get another offer from a third party, namely an attorney, who is attempting to interfere with your private contract, then you must recognize this new offer as a "separate" offer. You cannot "add" the attorney to the first contract as this is a different matter and it also does not properly notice him as you have started your first contract before the third party interfered. Let us define some terms before continuing.

Trespass. An unlawful interference with one's person, property, or rights. Any unauthorized intrusion or invasion or private premises or land of another. Trespass comprehends any misfeasance, transgression or offense which damages another person's health, reputation or property.

Criminal trespass. Criminal trespass is entering or remaining upon or in any land, structure, vehicle, aircraft or watercraft by one who knows he is not authorized or privileged to do so; and (a) He enters or remains therein in defiance of an order not to enter or to leave such premises or property personally communicated to him by the owner thereof or other authorized person; or (b) Such premises or property are posted in a manner reasonable likely to come to the attention of intruders, or a fenced or otherwise enclosed.

Interfere. To check; hamper; hinder; infringe; encroach trespass; disturb; intervene; intermeddle; interpose. To enter into, or to take part in, the concerns of others.

Interference with contractual relationship. This tort has four elements: existence of valid contract, defendant's knowledge of that contract, defendant's intentional procuring of breach of that contract and damages.

Entry. Practice means to place anything before court, or upon or among records, and is nearly equivalent to setting down formally in writing, either in full or abridged form but it may be used as meaning supply to file or duly deposit. In criminal law, entry is the unlawful making one's way into a dwelling or other house, for the purpose of committing a crime therein. In cases of burglary, the least entry with the whole or any part of the body, hand, or foot, or with any instrument or weapon, introduced for the purpose of committing a felony, is sufficient to complete the offense.

Dwell. [ME dwellen to lead astray, stun, abide, dwellan go astray, hinder] to live or stay as a permanent resident, reside; to linger over, emphasize, or ponder in thought, speech, or writing; to be motionless for a certain interval during operation.

Instrument. A formal legal document in writing, such as a contract, deed, will, bond, or lease. A writing that satisfies the requisites of negotiability prescribed by UCC Article 3. A negotiable instrument or any other writing which evidences a right to the payment of money and is not itself a security agreement...

If you happen to get an "instrument" in the mail from a third party which has "entered the dwelling" of the strawman that "evidences a right to payment of money" (such as a letter from an attorney) then it is time to accept his offer and create a contract with the intruder.

Maintenance. Lawsuits. An officious intermeddling in a lawsuit by a non-party by maintaining, supporting or assisting either party, with money or otherwise, to prosecute or defend the litigation.

Barratry. The offense of frequently exiting and stirring up quarrels and suits, either at law or otherwise. In maritime law, an act committed by master (magistrate) or mariners (attorneys) of a vessel (your strawman) for some fraudulent or unlawful purpose contrary to their duty (as a trustee) to owner (you) and resulting in injury to owner.

1. CREATING THE CONTRACT

1.   Notice of Acceptance to Contract
2.   Notice of Default
3.   Notice of Dishonor – from Notary Public
4.   Certificate of Dishonor - from Notary Public
5.   Default

The following steps are sequence of events that must occur to get your Contract established and enacted as the supreme law of the land.

1.   NOTICE OF ACCEPTANCE TO CONTRACT

Word process the Notice of Acceptance to Contract for all of the correct information

Print the Notice of Acceptance to Contract out, read it several times for correctness. Stamp the OFFER with your Acceptance for Value stamp and sign it. Then get the Notice notarized. Send the Notice of Acceptance to Contract by registered mail, return receipt so you have proof that they received your Contract you are in the process of creating. Send the copies of the above documents to the Respondent(s) and keep the originals

2.   NOTICE OF DEFAULT

After the 10 days send them a Notice of Fault. This notice completes your court procedure as a sovereign in your nation that is foreign to the public venue. Now you will need to pursue this matter in the "public venue" in their legal proceedings, however it will not go into the courts you are familiar with. You must take this matter up with the SECRETARY OF STATE of the state you are in.

Secretary of State. In American law. Title of the chief of the executive bureau of the United States called the "Department of State." He is a member of the cabinet, and is charged with the general administration of the international and diplomatic affairs of the government. In many of the state governments there is an executive officer bearing the same title and exercising important functions. In English law. The secretaries of state are cabinet ministers attending the sovereign for the receipt and dispatch of letters, grants, petitions, and many of the most important affairs of the kingdom, both foreign and domestic. Black's 4th edition

You are a foreign nation in their eyes, so you must go through the proper channels so that you can utilize the functions and duties of the Secretary of State – "general administration of the international affairs" and "attending the sovereign." There are many "designees" of the Secretary of the state in the area you live, normally called Notary Publics. Find a private Notary Public that you can work with; OR create one by getting a friend to become a Notary who understands this procedure.

3.   NOTICE OF DISHONOR – Notary Public

Now we will go through the process called a Notarial Protest, a very powerful process that will create a witness against the debtor through a Public Official. Following is the definition of a Notary Public according to Black's Law Dictionary, 6th edition. It is important to know why you need to use a Notary Public.

Notary Public: A public officer whose function it is to administer oaths; to attest and certify, by her or his hand and official seal, certain classes of documents, in order to give them credit and authenticity in foreign jurisdictions; to take acknowledgements of deeds and other conveyances, and certify the same; and to perform certain official acts, chiefly in commercial matters such as the protesting of notes and bills, the noting of foreign drafts, and marine protests in cases of loss or damage. One who is authorized by the State or Federal Government to administer oaths, and to attest to the authenticity of signatures. Black's 6th edition

Pursuant to Arizona Revised Statutes (ARS) Title 41-332;

Secretary of the State; deputy county clerk; county clerk functions
"…each clerk of the superior court shall deputize the secretary of state and the secretary's designees as deputy county clerks of the superior court solely for the performance of the superior court clerk's functions…"

In summary of the above definitions, a Notary Public is a commissioner designated by the secretary of the state and deputized to be a deputy superior court clerk to hear certain issues presented to them by foreign agents by taking depositions of the parties termed "notes." In order for the "notes" (contracts) to be binding they are registered in the public record.

4.   CERTIFICATE OF DISHONOR – Notary Public

If in 10 days the Notary Public does not receive a response point for point by affidavit with documented evidence, the debtor has defaulted and therefore dishonored your acceptance. Then the Notary prepares a Notarial Protest which the Notary keeps for her/his own records, and issues you a Certificate of Dishonor. The Certificate of Dishonor is similar to a Default Judgment in a Superior Court.

5.   DEFAULT

Now that you have a Default in your private venue and a Default in the public venue and the Respondent has assented to the terms and conditions by his silence, the Respondent has become your Debtor. You can now liquidate the Debtor's property.

You will write the DEFAULT in affidavit form summarizing the actions of what you have done to this point. The purpose for this document is to enter this matter into the public record so that one may begin to "foreclose or otherwise enforce the claim" which at this point will be liquidation.

UCC 9-601. Rights After Default;
(a) [Rights or secured party after default.] After default, a secured party has the rights provided in this part and except as otherwise provided in Section 9-602, those provided by agreement of the parties. A secured party:
1.   may reduce a claim to judgment, foreclose, or otherwise enforce the claim, security interest, or agricultural lien by any available judicial procedure; and UCC 9-607. Collection and Enforcement by Secured Party.
(b) [Nonjudicial enforcement of mortgage.] If necessary to enable a secured party to exercise under subsection (a)(3) the right of a debtor to enforce a mortgage nonjudicially, the secured party may record in the office in which a record of the mortgage is recorded:
1.   a copy of the security agreement that creates or provides for a security interest in the obligation secured by the mortgage; and
2.   the secured party's sworn affidavit in recordable form stating that:
a.   a default has occurred; and
b.   the secured party is entitled to enforce the mortgage nonjudicially.

Your contract is the "security agreement." The affidavit, entitled NOTICE OF DEFAULT, is the "sworn affidavit in recordable form stating that a default has occurred."

UCC 9-609. Secured Party's Right to Take Possession After Default.
    (a) [Possession; rendering equipment unusable; disposition on debtor's premises.] After default, a secured party:
1.   may take possession of the collateral;
    (b) [Judicial and nonjudicial process.] A secured party may proceed under subsection (a):
    (2) without judicial process, if it proceeds without breach of the peace.

Now that you have completed your "nonjudicial process," you can collect the collateral and take possession of it

John Henry Doe
c/o P.O. Box 5472
Tucson, AZ 85734

Contract No 92501-JHD

Robert W. Burns, d.b.a.

Attorney for Shakedown Law Firm
105 E Speedway
Phoenix, Arizona 85684
Respondent

NOTICE OF ACCEPTANCE TO CONTRACT

North Carolina)
NOTICE TO AGENT IS NOTICE TO PRINCIPAL
) ss
NOTICE TO PRINCIPAL IS NOTICE TO AGENT
Freedom County)

I, John Henry Doe, hereinafter "Secured Party", am competent to state the matters included in this contract which are true, correct and complete, and not meant to mislead.

STATEMENT OF FACTS

1) On September 15, 2014, Secured Party sent a documentary draft to Shyster Bank for adjustment and setoff. As professional banking agents, they knew or should have known that a collecting bank must follow documentary instructions or they are liable for the face value of the draft plus any damages that may have occurred.

2) On September 25, 2014, Secured Party received the documentary draft back to him by mail evidencing dishonor. The bank personnel did not follow instructions sent by Secured Party to process the transaction.

3) On October 11, 2014, Secured Party sent a NOTICE OF ERROR and REQUEST FOR INVESTIGATION to Debra N. Benda, d.b.a. VP of the Shyster Bank branch on 6257 E. Broadway. The notice requested Benda to follow banking laws specified in 15 USCA 1693(h) to initiate an investigation into this matter. Benda has not responded to the above request, which puts them in Default, and has now agreed to compensate Secured Party for $600,000.00 (Six hundred thousand Dollars).

4) On October 19, 2014, Secured Party received an offer from a third party to interfere and trespass on the private contract between Secured Party and Benda. The person who signed the offer to contract is Robert W. Burns, d.b.a. Attorney for Shyster Bank, hereinafter "Respondent".

5)   Secured Party hereby timely accepts the offer to contract from Respondent and herein state the terms and conditions.

TERMS AND CONDITIONS OF CONTRACT

6)   If Respondent chooses to trespass on or interfere, in any manner whatsoever, with the private contract between Baird and Secured Party, 03001-SWS-DNW, then he agrees to compensate Secured Party for $100,000.00 within ten (10) days.

7)   In the event respondent does not deliver $100,000.00 to Secured Party within ten (10) days as agreed to in this contract, Respondent agrees to compensate Secured Party for triple damages or $300,000.00 thereafter and may be subject to involuntary bankruptcy in his private capacity to settle the account.

8)   In the event Respondent withdraws his offer to contract within 10 days, then this contract will become void and Secured Party will not proceed with the enforcement of the above terms and conditions.

It has been said, so it is done.

Signed and sealed this _____ day of _____, 2015.
John Henry Doe
North Carolina   )
) ss
ACKNOWLEDGEMENT
Freedom County   )

As a Notary Public for said County and State, I do hereby certify that on this _____ day of _____
2015 the above mentioned appeared before me and executed the foregoing. Witness my hand and seal:

_____

_____
Notary Public
       My commission expires

John Henry Doe
c/o P.O. Box 5472
Tucson, AZ 85734

Contract No 92501-JHD
Robert W. Burns, d.b.a.
Attorney for Shakedown Law Firm
105 E Speedway
Phoenix, Arizona 85684
Respondent

NOTICE OF DEFAULT
North Carolina   )
NOTICE TO AGENT IS NOTICE TO PRINCIPAL
) ss
NOTICE TO PRINCIPAL IS NOTICE TO AGENT
Freedom County   )

Notice is hereby given, that the above named respondents are in Default upon the contract, entitled NOTICE OF ACCEPTANCE OF CONTRACT dated October 19, 2014, and therefore a Default has been entered upon them.

By the terms and conditions of the agreement contained in the Secured Party's affidavit, you were under obligation to timely and in good faith protest and make proper presentment with proof of your claim or interest. Your failure to do so is a dishonor and places you at Default.

By your default, you are deemed to be under the new terms and conditions of our original contract and have therefore waived all of your rights to your original presentment and terms. Any attempt to collect on your original presentment places you personally at risk for any damages incurred per this contract and may subject you to criminal sanctions and involuntary bankruptcy.

You are given ten (10) days to respond final judgment is made by sending an original affidavit to the specified Notary Public as a third party public official witness.

_____Date

_____
          John Henry Doe

NOTICE OF ASSENT

Robert W. Burns, d.b.a.
Attorney for Shakedown Law Firm
105 E Speedway
Freedom, Arizona 85684

Dear Mr. Burns,

I received a request to be a third party witness pursuant to Arizona Revised Statues at Sections 47-3505(a), from John Henry Doe, who informed me you have not responded to his acceptance to your offer to contract. The contents of the contract that he stated that he sent you consists of the NOTICE OF ACCEPTANCE TO CONTRACT, dated October 19, 2014, and NOTICE OF DEFAULT dated November 3, 2014. The notices were sent to you at 105 E Speedway, Freedom, Arizona 85684, as evidenced by U.S. Postal Service CERTIFICATE OF MAILING verifying the contents of the Mail package.
In the event your acquiescence was unintentional or due to reasonable neglect or impossibility, I am attaching a copy of the same presentment to this Notice.
You may respond to me, and I will forward your response to John Henry Doe. Your response is expected no later than ten (10) days from the postmark of this Notice of Assent.

Thank you for your prompt attention to this matter.

Sincerely,

_____
Notary Public (name)
Address:

_____
_____
_____

    (Stamp)

CERTIFICATE OF ASSENT

I, Diana L. Baker, am the notary to whom all communications are to be mailed regarding the contracts entitled NOTICE OF ACCEPTANCE TO CONTRACT, # 92501-JHD, herein "contract."

Pursuant to Arizona Revised Statutes 47-3505(b), and Uniform Commercial Code 3-505(b), Notice of Protest is hereby given with Certificate of Dishonor regarding the following:

On November 23, 2014, I mailed a Notice of Dishonor to Robert W. Burns, d.b.a. Attorney with Shakedown Law Firm, giving Respondent 10 days to answer.

As of this date, no response had been delivered to me, the designated receiver. I interviewed John Henry Doe, whose affidavit is attached to this Notarial Protest. John Henry Doe has stated to me by affidavit that Petitioner has received no response to said Contract at any other mailing location. Based on the foregoing information, Respondent has dishonored John Henry Doe's contract by non-acceptance and/or non-performance and have therefore assented to the terms and conditions in said Contract.

_____

Baker, Third Party Witness

Diana L.

Date_____

John Henry Doe
c/o P.O. Box 5472
Tucson, AZ 85734

Contract No 92501-JHD

Robert W. Burns, d.b.a.
Attorney for Shakedown Law Firm
105 E Speedway
Phoenix, Arizona 85684
Respondent

DEFAULT

North Carolina   )
NOTICE TO AGENT IS NOTICE TO PRINCIPAL
) ss
NOTICE TO PRINCIPAL IS NOTICE TO AGENT
Freedom County   )

The parties to the contract entitled, Notice of Acceptance to Contract, hereinafter "Contract", are in full agreement regarding the following:

1.   I, John Henry Doe, herein "Affiant", am competent to state to the matters included in this declaration, have knowledge of the facts, and declared that to the best of my knowledge, the statements made in this affidavit are true, correct, and not meant to mislead;

2.   Robert W. Burns is herein addressed in his private capacity, but in his public capacity is a citizen and resident of the State of Arizona and is participating in a commercial enterprise with his co-business partners, including but not limited to SHAKEDOWN LAW FIRM, hereinafter collectively referred to as "Respondent";

3.   The governing law of this private contract is the agreement of the parties supported by the Law Merchant and applicable maxims of law;

4.   Affiant at no time has willing, knowingly, intentionally, or voluntarily agreed to subordinate their position as creditor, through signature, words, actions, or inaction's;

5.   Affiant is not a party to a valid contract with Respondent that requires Affiant to perform in any manner, including but not limited to the payment of money to Respondent;

6.   On October 19, 2014, Secured Party received an offer from a third party to interfere and trespass on a private contract. The person who signed the offer to contract is Robert W. Burns, d.b.a. Attorney for Shyster Bank Loan Department, hereinafter "Respondent".

7.   On November 23, 2014, Diana L. Baker, a Public Notary, mailed a Notice of Dishonor to Robert W. Burns, d.b.a. Attorney with Shakedown Law Firm, giving Respondent 10 days to answer.

8.   On December 10, 2014, I received a Certificate of Assent from Diana L. Baker, the designated receiver for Respondent, stating that she had received no response from Respondent.

9.   Affiant sent Notices of Fault and Default allowing Respondent additional time to respond, however no response has been received so Respondent has fully agreed to all of the terms and conditions of the contract. Including the compensation to Affiant for a total of $300,000.00 (THREE HUNDRED THOUSAND DOLLARS).

It has been said, so shall it be done.

Dated this   day of   , 2014.

John Henry Doe
North Carolina   )
) ss
ACKNOWLEDGEMENT
Freedom County)

As a Notary Public for said County and State, I do hereby certify that on this _____ day of _____
2015 the above mentioned appeared before me and executed the foregoing. Witness my hand and seal:

_____
Notary Public

2. ENACTING THE CONTRACT

PURPOSE: The purpose of this procedure is to file and PERFECT the claim that you have against a debtor if they have dishonored you or your acceptance of their offer AND ENACT IT AS LAW. Before starting this process, one must have accepted all offers given to them, completed the administrative procedure, including the Notarial Protest, and now have a secured claim against the debtor. This procedure starts once you have a CERTIFICATE OF DISHONOR from the notary which is as valid as a Default Judgment in a Superior Court.

Bankrupt [L bank a bench + ruptus broken, literally one whose bench has been broken, the bench or table which a merchant or banker formerly used in the exchange having been broken on his bankruptcy.]
The Consolidated WEBSTER'S Encyclopedic Dictionary 1939 edition.

Bankrupt. Originally and strictly, a trader who secretes himself or does certain other acts tending to defraud his creditors. In a looser sense, an insolvent person. In English law there were two characteristics which distinguished bankrupts from insolvents; the former must have been a trader and the object of the proceedings against, not by him. As used in American law, the distinction between a bankrupt and an insolvent is not generally regarded.

Do you find it interesting that a "bankrupt" is one who acts to "defraud his creditors?" Who fits the description of a trader and who is the creditor?

Trader. One who makes it his business to buy merchandise, goods, or chattels to sell the same at a profit. One who sells goods substantially in the form in which they are bought; one who has not converted them into another form of property by his skill and labor.

The above definitions for "bankrupt" or "trader" could not be found in the Black's 6th edition and here is probably why. What institution do you know of "sells chattels substantially in the form in which they are bought?" Here is a hint – what does the bank do when they deposit your promissory note as an asset instead of a liability, then writes a check off of the deposit to give to the seller of the property? First of all, the bankers do not "buy" your credit with "money." After you GIVE your credit to them, they sell your credit to the seller of the property without "converting it into another form." It goes in and comes out the same – your credit! Or as they would say "money." Could this be considered of the bank to be an "act to defraud his creditor?"

Bankrupt Law. The leading distinction between a bankrupt law and an insolvent law, in the proper technical sense, consists in the character of the persons upon whom it is designed to operate, - the former contemplating as its objects bankrupts only, that is traders of a certain description; the latter insolvents in general, or persons unable to pay their debts. This has led to a marked separation between the two systems, in principle and in practice, which in England has always been carefully maintained, although the United States it has of late been disregarded. The only substantial difference between a strictly bankrupt law and an insolvent law lies in the circumstance that the former affords relief upon the application of the creditor, and the latter upon the application of the debtor.

Why do you think that United States has failed to maintain the difference between bankrupt and insolvency? I have a theory. Since they call you "bankrupt," they are "assuming" that you are acting to defraud your creditors and therefore you are in dishonor before walking into the court room, and that you are considered a "criminal" by the mere fact the you filed your bankruptcy petition.

Following is a step-by-step set of instructions that will assist you in your taking the equity from your debtors. Note, this is only an example that has been used to take property – one will still have to continue processes to KEEP IT! This procedure will, of course, be improved from time to time, but it is a good place to start.

Steps in Sequence

1. Notice of Substitution of Trustee
2. Collateral Found
3. Substitution of Trustee
4. UCC-1 assigned
5. Notice of Disposition
6. Disposition – Real Property
7. Disposition — Personal Property
8. Disposition — Vehicle
9. Confirmation of Receipt of Recordings and Filings

1. Notice of Substitution of Trustee

Information. An accusation exhibited against a person for some criminal offense, without an indictment. An accusation in the nature of an indictment, from which it differs only in being presented by a competent public officer on his oath of office, instead of a grand jury on their oath. Function of an "information" is to inform defendant of the nature of the charge made against him and the act constituting such charge so that he can prepare for trial and to prevent him from being tried again for the same offense. Black's Law Dictionary 6th edition

Notary Public. A public officer whose function it is to administer oaths; to attest and certify, by his hand and official seal, certain classes of documents, in order to give them credit and authenticity in foreign jurisdictions; the noting of foreign drafts.

Operating outside a bankruptcy proceeding is considered to be a crime according to 11 USCA. Any public official who is aware of an activity evidencing "unlawful operations" must report such activity to the "proper authorities" such as a US Attorney or the US Bankruptcy Trustee (Paul H. O'Neill). An information is an accusation exhibited by a "public official." Since a notary is a "public official" and has first hand knowledge of the crime by doing a Notarial Protest on that person, the notary must report such activities by "information." The information will be in the form of a "Certificate of Dishonor" issued by the notary that will include all previous notices and evidence of noticing that you have done since the beginning of the matter.

The information will be written by you and will contain all details and specifics on such activities and must be in affidavit form in order for a criminal complaint to be initiated and the matter investigated by the US Attorney or any other agency with a duty to handle the matter.

ACCEPTANCE SUPRA PROTEST (Acceptance for Honor). The acceptance or payment of a bill of exchange, after it has been dishonoured, by a person wishing to save the honour of the drawer or an endorser of the bill.

Dictionary of Business, Oxford University Press, © Market House Books Ltd 1996.

Supra Protest. In mercantile law. A term applied to an acceptance of a bill by a third person, after protest for nonacceptance by the drawee. Black's 4th edition

The second purpose for sending this document is to allow all of the notified parties an opportunity to "accept for honor" this matter. This package is to be sent to the Trustee of the UNITED STATES

Bankruptcy, Paul H. O'Neill, so they can investigate why the debtor is unlawfully using your exemption and operating outside the US Bankruptcy. If this third party (who represents you, the Creditor) does not wish to save the honor of the debtor (a sub-corporation or the U.S.), you will put the debtor into Involuntary Bankruptcy.

You will give a ten (10) day notice to the "proper authorities" in order to accept for honor or handle the situation. If they fail to respond, their silence is their consent for you to administrate and conclude the involuntary bankruptcy in a foreign proceeding – your court, as a foreign nation. This is pursuant to 11 USCA 303(b)(4). At this point, the state, United States or all of their agents can not come back to you and bring up the fact that you "did not have the authority" to liquidate the debtor's property.

The third purpose of this document is to give Paul H. O'Neill, the chapter 11 – Re-organization Bankruptcy Trustee, a notice of substitution. Being a chapter 11 trustee, he "fails to qualify" to commence with any chapter 7 – Liquidation proceedings so he must be "substituted" by another who is qualified to do so.

11 USCA 703 Successor trustee
(a) If a trustee dies or resigns during a case, fails to qualify under section 322 of this title or is removed under section 324 of this title, creditors may elect, in the manner specified in section 702 of this title, a person to fill the vacancy in the office of trustee.

Since the proceeding is foreign, you would not need a "person to fill the vacancy in the office of trustee," you would elect or assign a "private" trustee yourself.

Substitution. Putting in one person in the place of another; particularly, the act of a testator in naming a second devisee who is to take the bequest either on failure of the original devisee after him. Black's 4th edition

Testator. One who makes a Will.

Devisee. A person to whom lands or other real property are devised or given by will. In the case of a devise to an existing trust or trustee, or to a trustee on trust described by will, the trust or trustee is the devisee and the beneficiaries are not devisees.

Devise. A testamentary disposition of land or realty by the last will and testament of the donor; to dispose of real or personal property by will.

You may be asking "what does a will have to do with bankruptcy or trusts?" or "who died leaving you in charge anyway?"

One must remember that the debtor is a "trust" created by the state in order to keep an accounting of all the credit they are using in the creditor's name. It is just an account with the debtor showing how much the state or United States is liable to the creditor – the real man or woman.

The debtor is actually an unincorporated corporation (pursuant to 15 USCA 44) that has been operating in the public venue as a sub-corporation of UNITED STATES in a chapter 11 – Reorganization Bankruptcy. You as its creditor have allowed UNITED STATES and all its sub-corporations to operate in the bankruptcy on the condition that they must honor your method of payment per HJR 192. As creditor, your method of payment is a "set-off," or a cancellation of mutual debt. Their debt being interest due for the use of your credit that is backed by your property and your production. However, once the debtor dishonors your method of payment, then you may choose to "liquidate" the debtor by disposing all the property in the debtor's name. In other words "game over."

When the debtor is liquidated, that corporation "dies." Now the trust becomes a will and you have the superior claim to the property - unless the state wanted to bring their claim against the debtor! I would love to see them do that – they would have to admit to creating the strawman and consequently blow the lid off this whole scam.

After ten days with no response received regarding this matter, you will file a petition with the US Bankruptcy Court.

2.   Collateral Found and Listed

There are a number of ways to find collateral. The fastest and easiest way is to call an online private detective, the website is www.americafind.com. The phone number is 713-271-9518. For $99 the detective searches 22 databases to find the address, social security number, real property and other information of the Offeror. One can also go down to the Department of Motor Vehicles and tell them that you are going to place a lien on the Offeror's vehicle and that you need the

Vehicle Identification Number (V.I.N. number) for the lien. There are other detective services that are being tested and you can find your own methods by trial and error (one is Windsor Judicial Services). However, the main object of finding collateral is to find their social security number, address, real property and vehicle. List all the collateral as a separate attachment. An example of the specific descriptions is provided with theses instructions. The goal is to attach this list of collateral to a UCC-3 with the Offeror as the Debtor and claim it as your own property by filing it with the Secretary of State.

3.   Substitution of Trustee

This document substitutes Paul H. O'Neill, the chapter 11 – Reorganization Trustee, with the Chapter 7 – Liquidation Trustee. The substitution trustee will be named and an address given where to contact the trustee. This is a straight forward simple summary which will be attached to your UCC-1 when you file it along with the list of collateral.

4.   UCC-1 assigned

When you get the list of collateral done you are now ready to fill out a UCC-1. Fill-in the Debtors information and your information as the Secured Party in the appropriate boxes. The assignee, in section 5, who will receive the "Assignment for the benefit of Creditors" (you as the creditor), will be someone you know and trust. You will assign the collateral to the assignee, with the intent to dispose of it. The assignee is actually listed as an unincorporated foreign corporation, which is the strawman corporation of the flesh and blood being. This is a method of separating and using the strawman as an interface to the public venue, while remaining in the private side. This assignment is described more fully in Black's Dictionary, 6th Edition.

Assignment for benefit of creditors: A general assignment for benefit of creditors is transfer of all or substantially all of debtors property to another person in trust to collect any money owing to debtor, to sell property, to distribute the proceeds to his creditors and to return the surplus, if any, to debtor. Under Bankruptcy Act of 1898, such assignment was an "act of bankruptcy" if made within four months of bankruptcy.

Now that the UCC-1 has been filled out, attach the NOTICE OF SUBSTITUTION OF TRUSTEE, SUBSTITUTION OF TRUSTEE,

LIST OF COLLATERAL, CERTIFICATE OF DISHONOR and your NOTICE OF ACCEPTANCE TO CONTRACT with the DEFAULT. File these documents in the office of the secretary of the state, and then when you get your copy back from them, send a copy to the Debtor

     5.   Notice of Disposition

You must give the debtor at least a 10-day notification before you dispose of the property. Less is not considered a reasonable period of time. "Authenticated" in the definition below means notarized by a Notary Public and recorded at the County Recorders Office of the county the property is in.

UCC-9-611(b)[Notification of disposition required.] Except as otherwise provided in subsection (d), a secure party that disposes of collateral under Section 9-610 shall send to the persons specified in sub-section (c) a reasonable authenticated notice of disposition.

UCC-9-612(b)[10-day period sufficient in non-consumer transaction.] In a transaction other than a consumer transaction, a notification of disposition sent after default and 10 days or more before the earliest time of disposition set forth in the notification is sent within a reasonable time before the disposition.

Make a copy of the Notice of Disposition before you record it and send it to the Debtor giving him at least 10 days (21 to 30 days is better) notice to allow him a last chance remedy. Send this Notice by Certified Mail or any other proof of service.

     6.   Disposition – Real Property

The assignee you assigned in your UCC-1 has the duty to dispose of all the collateral that you find under the debtors name or is associated with the debtor.

Bill of Sale. In contracts, a written agreement, formerly limited to one under seal, by which one person assigns or transfers his right or interest in goods and personal chattels to another. Legal document which conveys title from seller to buyer

When one transfers title using a bill of sale it is actually the only real title that exists on the private side. This means that once you pay your property taxes with a closed checking account (substance) it takes the property out of the public side and a bill of sale is the only way it can be transferred privately. Any and every other form of title, i.e. deed of trust, warranty deed, etc. is a fiction and will transfer the private property back to the public side. The description of the real property should be in metes and bounds and township, section, and range if at all possible. Include the address and former property identification (tax I.D.) with a note that this is a fictional description.

However, if one is going to keep the property in the public, it is OK to file a Warranty Deed. Especially if you are going to transfer the property into a trust that you control.

7. Disposition — Personal Property

All other personal property will be transferred with a bill of sale or a UCC-3. Personal property may include BAR Licenses, business licenses, trade names, trademarks, copyrighted materials, bank accounts, computers and any other equipment.

8. Disposition — Vehicle

Vehicles will be transferred with a bill of sale and a transfer statement. Transfer statements are normally provided by the Department of Motor Vehicles. Request a transfer statement when you go to your DMV to register the vehicle and fill it out with the appropriate information. Present the transfer statement with the bill of sale at the DMV window and you will receive your new registration and plates.

9. Confirmation of Receipt of Recordings and Filings

This final step is to verify that all collateral is properly disposed of and titles transferred to their new owners.

John Henry Doe
c/o P.O. Box 5472
Tucson, AZ 85734

Contract No 92501-JHD

Robert W. Burns, d.b.a.
Attorney for Shakedown Law Firm
105 E Speedway
Phoenix, Arizona 85684
      Debtor

NOTICE OF SUBSTITUTION OF TRUSTEE

North Carolina   )

NOTICE TO AGENT IS NOTICE TO PRINCIPAL
) ss
NOTICE TO PRINCIPAL IS NOTICE TO AGENT
Freedom County   )

       I, John Henry Doe, herein "Creditor," hereby state that I am competent to make the following statements, have knowledge of the facts stated herein, that they are true, correct, complete and not meant to mislead and are presented in good faith:

1. The corporations, entitled UNITED STATES OF AMERICA, UNITED STATES, STATE OF ARIZONA, and above named, herein "Debtors," are Bankrupt and must operate pursuant to House Joint Resolution 192, June 5, 1933. The above corporations have been using the credit of Creditor since his birth, January 22, 1958, without remuneration to Creditor;

2. Creditor has accepted all offers and returned them to the above named Debtors thereby discharging all controversy and all charges. Debtors then claimed the charge still exists and therefore they are liable for the debt.

3. Creditor has accepted all offers and claims issued by Debtors and returned them to Debtors for proper processing. Debtors have failed to provide a remedy and is operating outside the UNITED STATES Bankruptcy – a criminal offense;

4. Debtors are holding the discharging instrument, but has failed to provide Creditor with a copy of the 1099 Original Issue Discount, therefore Debtors are TAX DELINQUENT since the claim is considered to be Creditor's exemption;

5. Creditor has timely noticed Debtors and has properly commenced and concluded a perfected security interest against Debtors. The perfected security interest, Contract No. 92501-JHD herein "Contract," includes all notices including a Certificate of Dishonor, herein "Information," issued by a Public Official.

TERMS AND CONDITIONS

6. John Snow, the chapter 11 bankruptcy trustee for the UNITED STATES, is hereby given a final opportunity to execute an Acceptance for Honor if he wishes to save the honor of the Debtors by giving Creditor a remedy. In the event John Snow does not wish to save the honor of Debtors, it will constitute John Snow's consent for substitution of trustee, whereas Creditor will designate an assignee of his choice to liquidate all of Debtor's property in a foreign proceeding pursuant to Contract #92501-JHD;

7.Debtor has ten (10) days from the date of postmark on this mailing to provide remedy regarding this matter. In the event Debtor fails to provide a remedy, Creditor will accept evidence of Debtors' dishonor as a refusal to volunteer into the bankruptcy remedy, whereby Debtors will be stripped of all immunity that UNITED STATES public policy may have otherwise afforded him. Upon dishonor, Debtors agrees in the alternative to Involuntary Bankruptcy that will be initiated on Debtors in a private capacity;

8.In the event Debtors dishonors, Debtors agrees to provide a list of all the property held in Debtors' names. Creditor will take the equity and place it for sale and proceed to liquidate the personal property for settlement of this account. Debtors additionally agrees to be placed on a UCC-1 Financing Statement as DEBTOR attaching it to a Declaration of Involuntary Bankruptcy and a list of Debtors' collateral. Upon filing the UCC-1 form with the Secretary of State of Arizona, the liquidation and disposition of property will be executed immediately.

Dated this _____ of _____, 2015.

_____
                John Henry Doe
North Carolina   )
) ss   ACKNOWLEDGEMENT
Freedom county   )

As a Notary Public for said County and State, I do hereby certify that on
this _____ day of_____
_____ the above mentioned appeared before me and executed the
foregoing. Witness my hand and seal:

_____
Notary Public

Copies forwarded to the following:

John Ashcroft
        John Snow
US Attorney General
        US Secretary of Treasury
950 Pennsylvania Avenue NW
        DEPARTMENT OF TREASURY
Washington, D.C. 20530-0001   1500
Pennsylvania Ave NW

        Washington D.C. 20220

Charles O. Rossotti
        Barack Obama
Internal Revenue Service, IRS   President
of the UNITED STATES
1111 Constitution Ave NW
        1600 Pennsylvania Avenue
Washington, DC 20224-0002
        Washington DC 20500

Norman Minetta   Tom
Ridge
US Secretary of Transportation   Director
of Homeland Security

400 Seventh Street, SW
Pennsylvania Avenue
Washington, DC 20590
    Washington DC 20500

1600

Colin L. Powell
Stafford
US Secretary of State
    Director of Secret Service
US Department of State
Government Service Agency
Washington, DC 20520-6810
    950 H Street, NW Ste 912

Washington, DC 20223

Brian L.

US

Jane Hull
    Betsey Bayless
Governor of the State of Arizona
Secretary of State
Arizona Executive Office of the Governor
Washington Street
1700 W. Washington Ave.
Arizona 85007
Phoenix, Arizona 85007

Arizona

1700 W.

Phoenix,

Janet Napolitano
Judicial Commission
Office of Attorney General
    1501 W. Washington
Department of Law
    Phoenix, AZ 85077
1275 W. Washington Street
Phoenix, Arizona 85007

Arizona

Barbara LaWall
Pima County Attorney
32 N. Stone Avenue, Ste 2100
Tucson, AZ 85701

Creditor:
John Henry Doe
c/o P.O. Box 5472
Tucson, AZ 85734

Debtor:
Robert W. Burns, d.b.a.
Attorney for Shakedown Law Firm
105 E Speedway
Phoenix, Arizona 85684

SUBSTITUTION OF TRUSTEE

Contract No 92501-JHD

North Carolina   )
NOTICE TO AGENT IS NOTICE TO PRINCIPAL
) ss
NOTICE TO PRINCIPAL IS NOTICE TO AGENT
Freedom County   )

I, John Henry Doe, herein "Creditor", hereby state that I am competent to make the following statements, have knowledge of the facts stated herein, that they are true, correct, complete and not meant to mislead and are presented in good faith:

The undersigned beneficiary hereby appoints WILLIAM HANSON HARRISON, an unincorporated foreign corporation, successor chapter 7 trustee under the contract #92501-JHD executed by ROBERT W. BURNS as Debtor, in which John Henry Doe is named as Creditor, and under the contract/treaty 100701-SWS whereby John Snow is named as the chapter 11 trustee of the UNITED STATES Bankruptcy.

      WHEREAS, the undersigned is the present Creditor under said contracts and,
      WHEREAS, the undersigned desires to substitute a new Trustee under said
Contract in the place and stead of said original Trustee there under.

NOW, THEREFORE, the undersigned hereby substitutes WILLIAM HANSON HARRISON, an unincorporated foreign corporation, PMB 278, 1830 East Broadway Ste 124, Tucson, AZ 85734

Dated this ____ of _____, 2015.

_____
      John Henry Doe, Creditor

For the purpose of verification of signature -- and seal -- and for public
notice, I the undersigned Notary Public, being commissioned in the
county noted above, do declare on the _____ day of _____
2015, the one known to me to be, or who proved to me to be John
Henry Doe did execute this document before me.

_____

               _____
Notary Public

        My Commission expires

When recorded mail to: William Hanson Harrison
                     PMB 278, 1830 East Broadway Ste 124
      Tucson, AZ 85734

NOTICE OF DISPOSITION

North Carolina   )
NOTICE TO AGENT IS NOTICE TO PRINCIPAL
) ss
NOTICE TO PRINCIPAL IS NOTICE TO AGENT
Freedom County   )

I, William Hanson Harrison, agent for WILLIAM HANSON HARRISON, an unincorporated foreign corporation, hereinafter "Grantor", am competent to state the matters included in this contract which are true, correct and complete, and not meant to mislead.

Grantor has been designated to execute the ASSIGNMENT FOR THE BENEFIT OF CREDITOR pursuant to the Involuntary Bankruptcy as stated in Contract No 92501-JHD in the UCC-1 Financing Statement filed June 3, 2015 with the Secretary of State of Arizona for

Secured Party: John Henry Doe
               PO Box 34567,   Tucson, AZ 85734   Phone: (520) 465-1111

Grantor: WILLIAM HANSON HARRISON, an unincorporated foreign corporation
               PMB 278, 1830 East Broadway Ste 124,   Tucson, AZ 85734

DEBTOR: ROBERT W. BURNS, d.b.a. Attorney for Shakedown Law Firm
               105 E Speedway, Phoenix, AZ 85684

Interested Party: John Snow, d.b.a. Trustee for U.S. Bankruptcy
            1500 Pennsylvania Ave NW
            Washington D.C. 20220

the following described Real Property Located in PIMA, Arizona

CASAS BONITAS LOT 6, BLOCK B, BOOK 8 OF MAPS PLATS AT PAGE 28
Recorded 03/10/89 at Docket 8491, Page 381,

At the Address of : 105 E Speedway, Phoenix, AZ 85684
PARCEL NUMBER 125-09-1760

We will sell the described property privately in 11 days, sometime after August 12, 2015. You are entitled to an accounting of the unpaid indebtedness secured by the property that we intend to sell. You may request an accounting by calling us at (303) 230-4919.

_____

WILLIAM HANSON HARRISON, an unincorporated foreign corporation

BY: William Hanson Harrison, Creditor
North Carolina   )
) ss
ACKNOWLEDGEMENT
Freedom County)

As a Notary Public for said County and State, I do hereby certify that on this _____day of_____
_____ the above mentioned appeared before me and executed the foregoing. Witness my hand and seal:

_____

Notary Public

When recorded mail to: JOHN SMITH
                          342 E Broadway
                          Tucson, Arizona 85746

Contract No 92501-JHD

WARRANTY DEED

For the consideration of TEN AND NO/100 DOLLARS, and other valuable considerations, I or we,

WILLIAM HANSON HARRISON, an unincorporated foreign corporation
PMB 278, 1830 East Broadway Ste 124,   Tucson, AZ 85734

> GRANTOR do hereby convey to

JOHN SMITH
342 E Broadway
Tucson, Arizona 85746
> GRANTEE the following described Real Property Located in
PIMA, Arizona

CASAS BONITAS LOT 6, BLOCK B, BOOK 8 OF MAPS PLATS AT PAGE 28
Recorded 03/10/89 at Docket 8491, Page 381,
At the Address of : 105 E Speedway, Phoenix, AZ 85684
FORMER TAX IDENTIFICATION NUMBER 125-09-1760

SUBJECT TO: Existing taxes, assessments, liens, encumbrances, covenants conditions, restrictions, Rights of way and easements, and obligations and liabilities of record.

And the GRANTOR does warrant the title against all persons whomsoever, subject to the matters above set forth.

Transferred this _____Day of _____, 2015.

_____
WILLIAM HANSON HARRISON, an unincorporated foreign corporation

> BY: William Hanson Harrison, Creditor

For the purpose of verification of signature -- and seal -- and for public notice, I the undersigned Notary Public, being commissioned in the county noted above, do declare on the _____ day of _____ 2015, the one known to me to be, or who proved to me to be William Hanson Harrison did execute this document before me.

_____

Notary Public

_____
My Commission expires

When recorded mail to: JOHN SMITH
                         342 E Broadway
                         Tucson, Arizona 85746

BILL OF SALE AND CONTRACT FOR DEED

For the consideration of TEN AND NO/100 DOLLARS, and other valuable considerations, I or we,

WILLIAM HANSON HARRISON, an unincorporated foreign corporation
PMB 278
1830 East Broadway Ste 124
Tucson, AZ 85734
        GRANTOR do hereby convey to

JOHN SMITH
342 E Broadway
Tucson, Arizona 85746
        GRANTEE without covenant or warranty, express or implied, all right, title and interest of Grantor in Real Property in allodium. Pursuant to the Declaration of Involuntary Bankruptcy, Real Property was sold by Grantor at Bankruptcy Liquidation on June 19, 2002, at a private sale to Grantee who was the transferee for Real Property, for $94,000.00, which will be paid with $10,000.00 Down and monthly principal payments of $1,000.00 per month for eighty-four (84) months (7 years) with 0% interest.

the following formerly described Real Property Located in PIMA, Arizona

CASAS BONITAS LOT 6, BLOCK B, BOOK 8 OF MAPS PLATS AT PAGE 28
Recorded 03/10/89 at Docket 8491, Page 381,
At the Address of : 105 E Speedway, Phoenix, AZ 85684
FORMER TAX IDENTIFICATION NUMBER 125-09-1760

Grantee is now the owner of the land and property described above which is now private property exempt from levy and not under the jurisdiction of anyone or any artificial entity.

Transferred this _____Day of _____, 2003.

_____
WILLIAM HANSON HARRISON, an unincorporated foreign corporation

BY: William Hanson Harrison, Creditor
North Carolina   )
) ss
ACKNOWLEDGEMENT
Freedom County)

As a Notary Public for said County and State, I do hereby certify that on this _____ day of _____
_____ the above mentioned appeared before me and executed the foregoing. Witness my hand and seal:

_____
Notary Public

WILLIAM HANSON HARRISON
an unincorporated foreign corporation
PMB 2781830 East Broadway Ste 124
Tucson, AZ 85734

BILL OF SALE

To Whom It May Concern:

For receipt of the sum of $5,000.00, WILLIAM HANSON HARRISON does hereby sell and transfer at a Bankruptcy Liquidation Sale the motor vehicle described as;

Make: Toyota
Model: Camry
Year: 1999
VIN: 3994837237292200

To: JOHN SMITH
            342 E Broadway
Tucson, Arizona 85746

Transferred this _____ day of _____ 2015.

_____
WILLIAM HANSON HARRISON, an unincorporated foreign corporation

            BY: William Hanson Harrison, Creditor

Arizona   )
) ss   ACKNOWLEDGEMENT
Pima county   )

As a Notary Public for said County and State, I do hereby certify that on this _____ day of _____
_____ the above mentioned appeared before me and executed the foregoing. Witness my hand and seal:

_____
Notary Public

3. EXECUTING YOUR CONTRACT

PURPOSE: The purpose of this procedure is to execute the claim that you have against a debtor in order to get you equity back. Before starting this process, one must have properly filed with your agent the Secretary of State and consequently now have a perfected secured claim against the debtor. This procedure starts after you have recorded a NOTICE OF DISPOSITION and sent the Debtor a copy of it giving them ten (10) days before the Liquidation Sale and then transferred the property.

Execute. To complete; to make; to sign; to perform; to do; to follow out; to carry out according to its terms; to fulfill the command or purpose of.

This "eviction" process is the same one that the bank uses to remove people who do not know they are Creditors from their homes. We have taken the same documents they have sent us and are using them to evict the bankers from their own buildings! Is this a great country or what?

The following documents will be used in this process:

1.   NOTICE REQUIRING DELIVERY OF POSSESSION OF PREMISES
2.   SERVICE OF PROCESS BY PRIVATE PERSON
3.   LETTER OF ACKNOWLEDGEMENT
4.   SUMMONS FOR FORCIBLE ENTRY AND DETAINER
5.   COMPLAINT IN FORCIBLE ENTRY AND DETAINER
6.   AFFIDAVIT FOR APPLICATION FOR DEFAULT JUDGMENT
7.   ENTRY FOR DEFAULT
8.   DEFAULT JUDGMENT

1.   NOTICE REQUIRING DELIVERY OF POSSESSION OF PREMISES

After you have transferred title to another person, they will have to evict the tenants from the property.

Eviction. Dispossession by process of law; the act of depriving a person of the possession of land or rental property which he has held or leased. Act of turning a tenant out of possession, either by re-entry or legal proceedings, such as an action of ejectment.

Re-entry. The act of resuming the possession of lands or tenements in pursuance of a right which party exercising it reserved to himself when he quit his former possession. The right reserved by a grantor to enter the premises on breach of a condition of the conveyance.

Quit. To leave; remove from; surrender possession of; as when a tenant "quits" the premises or receives a "notice to quit."

Remember the quote from the 73rd Congress, March 9, 1933: "It (the new money) will be worth 100 cents on the dollar, because it is backed by the credit of the Nation. It will represent a mortgage on all the homes and other property of all the people in the Nation."

You see, we as Creditors have given our homes, property and substance up to UNITED STATES to be mortgaged so that they can operate in the bankruptcy. When any agent in UNITED STATES breaches the "mortgage" then we can claim RE-ENTRY and enter the premises that we "quit" when we "surrendered the possession" of the property to the state originally in 1933. It does not matter if it is the same property, it matters that whenever an agent for UNITED STATES (our Debtor) breaches the contract we can claim "possession" of the property back.

2.   SERVICE OF PROCESS BY PRIVATE PERSON

Service of Process can be done by a private person in the state of Arizona. You will have to check to see if this is legal in your state. The reason why this is so important in this case is that you will be going to court and this will be a requirement to have legal service of process. The process server can be anyone you know, but not a relative. They only need to serve the address if no one is present to answer the door.

This process has nothing to do with serving the person – only the address. I know this for a fact as I had a house that I rented out and I never got the document that was served on the "tenants." You see it is not the person occupying the property that matters, only the address that is served.

3.   LETTER OF ACKNOWLEDGEMENT

After 7 days go back to the house and if they have vacated send John Snow the Trustee to the US Bankruptcy a LETTER OF ACKNOWLEDGEMENT acknowledging the delivery of the possession of the premises to the owner. Why John Snow, you might be asking? Because he is an agent of the US who manages the bankruptcy for you and you let him know that this property is no longer in the possession of UNITED STATES.

1.   SUMMONS FOR FORCIBLE ENTRY AND DETAINER

If however, the "tenants" are detaining you from possession your property, you will start an eviction process to remove them. The summons will notify them of when they will have to answer or they will be in Default.

2.   COMPLAINT IN FORCIBLE ENTRY AND DETAINER

Forcible entry and detainer. A summary proceeding for restoring to possession of land by one who is wrongfully kept out or has been wrongfully deprived of the possession. An action to obtain possession or repossession of real property which had been transferred from one to another pursuant to contract; such proceeding is not an action to determine ownership of title to property.

How many times have we went to court thinking "we will just bring up all the paperwork we have sent them about ownership and title of the house?" So what did we learn when that did not work? Did we ever look up the meaning of this action? Nooooooooooo! We just complained and blamed the system.

You see, this action has nothing to do with "ownership of title to property." In fact, you cannot even bring it up as some of you have tried and gotten "denied." This action is about TENANCY and only that. So when you walk into court, how do you think the judge and the bank attorney look at you? You got it – a tenant!

There is only one thing that can be brought up in that court room – do you have a lease agreement or not. No one that I know has ever had a lease with the bank because they "assigned" the lease to the bank when they signed the Deed of Trust (no kidding)! So when the "tenant" cannot provide a lease, he is given an arbitrary time to remove himself from the premises. He is also told how much rent he is being charged with per day – now he really is a tenant.

Since this works so well on us, it will work on them. When you evict the bank, it will not matter how many attorneys they bring into the courtroom – THEY CAN NEVER BRING UP OWNERSHIP OF THE TITLE TO THE PROPERTY!!!!! Use their own instruments against them. Is that justice or what?

3. AFFIDAVIT FOR APPLICATION FOR DEFAULT JUDGMENT

After 20 days (30 days for out of state) and you do not get an answer from the tenants, they have defaulted and you can file for a Default Judgment. This must be in affidavit form summarizing what has been done to this point. You will also file the ENTRY FOR DEFAULT for the Clerk of the Court to sign, and the DEFAULT JUDGMENT for the judge to sign.

4.   ENTRY FOR DEFAULT

This document is written up by you as if the Clerk of the Court was writing it. The clerk will verify that no response or answer has been made by Defendants, then the clerk will issue a NOTICE OF DEFAULT to the Defendant giving them 10 additional days to answer. If Defendants do not answer within 10 days, the clerk will take this to the judge or even issue the Default themselves.

5.   DEFAULT JUDGMENT

Since there has been no response from the Defendants, the judge will have no choice but to issue the DEFAULT JUDGMENT in your favor. Now the clerk will issue a "Writ of Restitution" to the Sheriff to evict the tenants from your property.

JOHN SMITH
342 E Broadway
Tucson, Arizona 85746

NOTICE REQUIRING DELIVERY OF POSSESSION OF PREMISES

TO: ROBERT W. BURNS, d.b.a. Attorney for Shakedown Law Firm
AND ALL OCCUPANTS, TENANTS OR SUBTENANTS
POSSESSION OF PREMISES LOCATED AT:
     105 E Speedway
     Phoenix, AZ 85684

NOTICE IS HEREBY GIVEN that, John Smith has purchased the above described property at a liquidation sale under Involuntary Bankruptcy proceedings by Notice of Disposition and transferred by a Bill of Sale duly recorded.

NOTICE IS FURTHER GIVEN that within seven (7) days after the service of this NOTICE upon you, you are required to deliver up possession of the above described premises to the undersigned, or legal proceedings will be commenced against you to recover possession of said premises.

This NOTICE is given to you pursuant to Section 12-1171 through 12-1174 of the Arizona Revised Statutes. For further information, please contact Wade at (303) 883-3556.

DATED THIS: _____, 2015

OWNER: _____.

John Smith

JOHN SMITH
342 E Broadway
Tucson, Arizona 85746

FREEDOM COUNTY, STATE OF ARIZONA

John Smith   )
)
                        vs   )
)
ROBERT W. BURNS, d.b.a. Attorney for   )
SHAKEDOWN LAW FIRM   )
AND ALL OCCUPANTS, TENANTS OR   )
SUBTENANTS   )
POSSESSION OF PREMISES LOCATED AT:)
SERVICE OF PROCESS
105 E Speedway   )
BY PRIVATE PERSON
Phoenix, AZ 85684   )
_____)

I declare that I am a citizen of the United States, over the age of eighteen, and not a party to this action. And that within the boundaries of the state where service was affected, I was authorized to perform said service.

On August 14, 2015, I received a document entitled, NOTICE REQUIRING DELIVERY OF POSSESSION OF PREMISES.

Copies of which I personally served as follows:
UPON OCCUPANT, BY SERVING ONE TRUE COPY UPON JOHN DOE RESIDING THEREIN, AT THE ADDRESS OF 9322 South Patricia Drive, Tucson, FREEDOM COUNTY, Arizona 85746, AT THE HOUR OF 11:15 AM.

TOTAL COST OF SERVICE: $25.00

_____

William Smith

North Carolina)

) ss

ACKNOWLEDGEMENT
Freedom County)

As a Notary Public for said County and State, I do hereby certify that on
this _____ day of _____
_____ the above mentioned appeared before me and executed the
foregoing. Witness my hand and seal:

_____
Notary Public

John Smith
342 E Broadway
Tucson, Arizona 85746

LETTER OF ACKNOWLEDGEMENT

TO: John Snow, d.b.a. Trustee for U.S. Bankruptcy
1500 Pennsylvania Ave NW
Washington D.C. 20220

ACKNOWLEDGEMENT IS HEREBY GIVEN that ROBERT W.
BURNS and ALL OCCUPANTS, TENANTS OR SUBTENANTS,
herein "Tenants", have vacated and have delivered up possession of the
above-described premises to the undersigned owner of the property, John
Smith.

NOTICE IS FURTHER GIVEN that, at anytime in the future, Tenants or
any agent thereof wishing to enter the property, a request in writing to
John Smith will be required 10 days in advance. Permission will be
granted upon the discretion of the owner. If forcible entry is made by
Tenants from this point forward legal proceedings will be commenced
against them to recover possession of said premises.

Tenants are thanked for their cooperation in this matter.

DATED THIS: _____, 2015

OWNER:_____

John Smith

John Smith
342 E Broadway
Tucson, Arizona 85746

ARIZONA SUPERIOR COURT

FREEDOM COUNTY

JOHN SMITH	)
	)
CASE NO._____	
Plaintiff,	)
	)
SUMMONS	
Vs.	)
	)
FORCIBLE ENTRY	
ROBERT W. BURNS, d.b.a. Attorney for	)
AND DETAINER	
SHAKEDOWN LAW FIRM.)	
AND ALL OCCUPANTS, TENANTS OR	)
SUBTENANTS	)
POSSESSION OF PREMISES LOCATED AT:)	
105 E Speedway	)
Phoenix, AZ 85684	)
& DOES I - X inclusive,	)
	)
Defendants	)
_____)	

THE STATE OF ARIZONA TO:
ROBERT W. BURNS, d.b.a. Attorney for Shakedown Law Firm
AND ALL OCCUPANTS, TENANTS OR SUBTENANTS & DOES I -
X inclusive

YOUR ARE HEREBY SUMMONED and required to appear and defend
or answer in this action in this Court as follows: ARS ss12-1175

    BEFORE: _____
DATE AND TIME: _____
PLACE: Division No. _____of this Court located at:

_____

You are further advised that Plaintiffs seek to recover possession of the following property:
105 E SPEEDWAY, PHOENIX, AZ 85684

YOU ARE HEREBY NOTIFIED that in case of your failure to appear and defend within the time applicable, judgment by default may be rendered against you for the relief demanded in the Complaint.

REQUESTS FOR REASONABLE ACCOMODATION FOR PERSONS WITH DISABILITIES MUST BE MADE TO THE COURT BY PARTIES AT LEAST 3 WORKING DAYS IN ADVANCE OF A SCHEDULED COURT PROCEEDING.

SIGNED, SEALED AND DATED_____,
2015.

CLERK OF THE COURT

    BY:_____

Deputy Clerk

ORIGINAL FILED:

COPY of the foregoing sent
_____ day of May, 2002 to:

ROBERT W. BURNS
105 E Speedway
Phoenix, AZ 85684

John Snow, d.b.a. Trustee for U.S. Bankruptcy
1500 Pennsylvania Ave NW
Washington D.C. 20220

John Smith
342 E Broadway
Tucson, Arizona 85746

ARIZONA SUPERIOR COURT

FREEDOM COUNTY

JOHN SMITH	)
	) CASE
NO._____	
Plaintiff,)	
	)
Vs.	)
COMPLAINT IN	
	)
FORCIBLE ENTRY	
ROBERT W. BURNS, d.b.a. Attorney for)	AND DETAINER
SHAKEDOWN LAW FIRM	)
AND ALL OCCUPANTS, TENANTS OR)	
SUBTENANTS)	
POSSESSION OF PREMISES LOCATED AT:)	
105 E Speedway)	
Phoenix, AZ 85684	)
& DOES I - X inclusive,)	
	)
Defendants)	

Plaintiff alleges:

PARTIES AND JURISDICTION

1.   Plaintiff is a Creditor registered to do business in Arizona and is entitled to the possession of, and is the recorded owner of a parcel of property and the dwelling thereon located at: 105 E Speedway, Phoenix, AZ 85684, property is more particularly described as follows:

CASAS BONITAS LOT 6, BLOCK B, BOOK 8 OF MAPS PLATS AT PAGE 28, RECORDS OF PIMA COUNTY, ARIZONA as located within the above-captioned Judicial District and County.

2. The true names or capacities, whether individual, corporate, associate or otherwise of the Defendants named herein as DOES I through X in occupancy are unknown to Plaintiff, who therefore sues said Defendants by such fictitious names.

Plaintiff will amend this complaint to show their true names and capacities when they have been ascertained.

3. That Defendants, and each of them, are currently in possession of and occupying the above-described real property.

CAUSE OF ACTION FOR FORCIBLE DETAINER

4. The Plaintiff purchased the above-described real property at a Liquidation

Sale held on July 21, 2014, in accordance with Arizona Revised Statutes Section 47-9612 and 47-9613 et seq. and its title has been duly perfected.

5. That Plaintiff has a duly executed Bill of Sale and Contract for Deed, a copy of which is attached hereto as Exhibit "A" and by this reference incorporated herein as if set forth in full.

6. That on July 27, 2014, by written notice, and in compliance with Arizona Revised Statutes Section 12-1173.01, Plaintiff made demand on said Defendants for and required the delivery of possession of said real property within seven (7) days from service of said notice, a copy of which is attached hereto as Exhibit "B" and by this reference, incorporated herein as if set forth in full.

7. Said written Notice and demand served upon the Defendants has been neglected and refused for seven (7) days following its service upon them, and remains neglected and refused now. A true copy of the Affidavit of Service of the Notice is attached hereto as Exhibit "C" and by this reference, incorporated herein as if set forth in full.

8. Said Defendants unlawfully are continuing in possession of said premises after said demand and without permission of the Plaintiff and under no claim of right.

9. The reasonable value for the use and occupancy of the subject premises is $30.00 per day. Plaintiff seeks such damages from July 21, 2014, the date of the Liquidation sale, and for each day thereafter, until the date Defendants are removed from the remises.

10. Plaintiff has performed all the necessary conditions and given all the required notices to bring this Forcible Detainer action.

WHEREFORE, Plaintiff requests for Judgment as follows:

1. Defendants be ordered to leave and vacate subject premises and Plaintiff be placed in possession thereof;

2. For an order to the Clerk of the Court to issue a Writ of Restitution, in this action to the Sheriff of Pima County, Arizona, commanding him to immediately restore possession of the property to Plaintiff from Defendants and all persons holding possession under Defendants or otherwise;

3. Defendants be ordered to pay a fair rental on the premises from July 21, 2014, through the date of judgment at the rate of $30.00 per day;

4. For such other relief as this Court may deem just and proper.

DATED_____, 2014.

BY:_____ John Smith
ORIGINAL FILED:

COPY of the foregoing sent
_____ day of May, 2014 to:

ROBERT W. BURNS
105 E Speedway
Phoenix, AZ 85684

John Snow, d.b.a. Trustee for U.S. Bankruptcy
1500 Pennsylvania Ave NW
Washington D.C. 20220

John Smith
342 E Broadway
Tucson, Arizona 85746

ARIZONA SUPERIOR COURT

FREEDOM COUNTY

JOHN SMITH   )
)   CASE
NO._____
        Plaintiff,   )
)
        AFFIDAVIT IN SUPPORT OF
        Vs.   )
)
        APPLICATION FOR
ROBERT W. BURNS, d.b.a. Attorney for   )
SHAKEDOWN LAW FIRM   )   ENTRY
OF DEFAULT
AND ALL OCCUPANTS, TENANTS OR)
SUBTENANTS   )
POSSESSION OF PREMISES LOCATED AT:)
105 E Speedway   )
Phoenix, AZ 85684   )
& DOES I - X inclusive,   )

)
                Defendants   )
_____)

North Carolina   )
) ss
Freedom County   )

        I, John Smith, herein "Plaintiff", hereby state that I am
competent to make the following statements, have knowledge of the facts

stated herein, that they are true, correct, complete and not meant to mislead and are presented in good faith:

On _____ Plaintiff filed with the Superior Court a cause entitled Forcible Entry and Detainer against Defendants ROBERT W. BURNS, d.b.a. Attorney for SHAKEDOWN LAW FIRM AND ALL OCCUPANTS, TENANTS OR SUBTENANTS and DOES I - X inclusive, herein "Defendants." Plaintiff is now filing for Application for Entry of Default on the Forcible Entry and Detainer and Affidavit in Support of Application for Entry of Default that Defendants have been regularly served with process, that Defendants have failed to plead or otherwise defend as to the complaint on file in this action, and the time allowed has expired, the default of Defendants is hereby applied for to the Clerk of the Superior Court. This default shall not be effective if Defendants plead or otherwise defend prior to the expiration of ten (10) days from the date hereof.

DATED_____, 2015.

_____

John Smith
North Carolina   )
)
ACKNOWLEDGEMENT
Wake County   )

For the purpose of verification of signature -- and seal -- and for public notice, I the undersigned Notary Public, being commissioned in the county noted above, do declare on the _____ day of _____ 2015, the one known to me to be, or who proved to me to be John Smith did execute this document before me.

_____

Notary Public
                  _____
                  My Commission expires

ORIGINAL FILED:

COPY of the foregoing sent
_____ day of May, 2015 to:

ROBERT W. BURNS
105 E Speedway
Raleigh, NC 85684

John Snow, d.b.a. Trustee for U.S. Bankruptcy
1500 Pennsylvania Ave NW
Washington D.C. 20220

John Smith
342 E Broadway
Raleigh, North Carolina 27601

NORTH CAROLINA SUPERIOR COURT

WILSON COUNTY

JOHN SMITH   )
)   CASE
NO._____
                 Plaintiff,   )
)   ENTRY
OF DEFAULT
              Vs.   )
)
ROBERT W. BURNS, d.b.a. Attorney for   )
SHAKEDOWN LAW FIRM.   )
AND ALL OCCUPANTS, TENANTS OR)
SUBTENANTS   )
POSSESSION OF PREMISES LOCATED AT:)
105 E Speedway   )
Raleigh, NC 27601   )
& DOES I - X inclusive,   )
)
              Defendants   )
_____)

It appearing to the Clerk of this Court from the Plaintiff's Application for Entry of

Default on the Forcible Entry and Detainer and Affidavit in Support of Application for

Entry of Default that Defendants ROBERT W. BURNS, d.b.a. Attorney for SHAKEDOWN LAW FIRM AND ALL OCCUMPANTS, TENTANTS , its successors and/ or assigns and DOES I - X inclusive, herein "Defendants", have been regularly served with process, that Defendants have failed to plead or otherwise defend as to the complaint on file in this action, and the time allowed has expired, the default of

Defendants is hereby entered. This default shall not be effective if Defendants pleads or otherwise defend prior to the expiration of ten (10) days from the date hereof.

SIGNED, SEALED AND DATED_____,
2015.

CLERK OF THE COURT

BY:_____

Deputy Clerk

ORIGINAL FILED:

COPY of the foregoing sent
_____ day of May, 2015 to:

ROBERT W. BURNS
105 E Speedway
Raleigh, NC 27601

John Snow, d.b.a. Trustee for U.S. Bankruptcy
1500 Pennsylvania Ave NW
Washington D.C. 20220

John Smith
342 E Broadway
Raleigh, North Carolina 27601

NORTH CAROLINA SUPERIOR COURT

WILSON COUNTY

JOHN SMITH   )
)   CASE
NO._____
          Plaintiff,   )
)
          Vs.   )
)
          DEFAULT   JUDGMENT
ROBERT W. BURNS, d.b.a. Attorney for   )
SHAKEDOWN LAW FIRM.   )
AND ALL OCCUPANTS, TENANTS OR   )
SUBTENANTS   )
POSSESSION OF PREMISES LOCATED AT:)
105 E Speedway   )
Raleigh, NC 27601   )
& DOES I - X inclusive,   )
)
          Defendants   )
_____)

This cause came regularly to the Superior Court on _____ .

Defendants, being properly served, failed to appear or otherwise respond
to the Complaint. The Court having considered the evidence before it and
finding that the Defendants herein named were regularly entered; that the
allegations contained in Plaintiff's Complaint are true and correct; and
there is no just reason for a delay in entering a final judgment against the
persons named below, and good cause appearing therefore:

IT IS HEREBY ORDERED, ADJUDGED AND DECREED that Plaintiff is granted Judgment against the Defendant, ROBERT W. BURNS, d.b.a. Attorney for SHAKEDOWN LAW FIRM AND ALL OCCUPANTS, TENANTS OR SUBTENANTS POSSESSION OF PREMISES LOCATED AT:& DOES I - X inclusive, and each of them as follows:

1.   For possessions of the premises located at 105 E Speedway, Phoenix, AZ 85684, and;

2.   Rental damages and costs are waived.

IT IS FURTHER ORDERED that should Defendants fail or refuse to vacate according to this Order, Plaintiff shall be entitled to the Issuance of a Writ of Restitution of the aforementioned premises no sooner than _____, 2015.

IT IS FURTHER ORDERED that this judgment be entered at this time as a final Judgment.

DATED_____, 2015.

_____Superior Court Judge/Commissioner

ORIGINAL FILED:

COPY of the foregoing sent
_____ day of May, 2002 to:

ROBERT W. BURNS
105 E Speedway
Raleigh, NC 27601

John Snow, d.b.a. Trustee for U.S. Bankruptcy
1500 Pennsylvania Ave NW
Washington D.C. 20220

THE APPEARANCE BOND

In the course of your business, one may eventually get a court order from one of your debtors to "argue" about the matter. There is no need to dishonor their offer to go to court, so just accept it or conditionally accept it to shift the burden of proof asking THEM to prove you are NOT the creditor. It is possible that the court may issue an "arrest warrant" to force you into agreeing with their point of view even though they have already dishonored. However, not to worry, there is a brilliant method of discharging this "charge." KNOWING the fact that, "you are the Creditor," firmly implanted in your mind, we will begin to define several key terms from this powerful viewpoint.

While defining the following terms, keep in mind how each definition relates to "accounting principles." The "court" is merely a commercial enterprise existing primarily to sell you "governmental services" such as "whisking you off to secluded get-a-ways" where you get "free room and board" and the "state of the art security is the finest money (your credit) can by." First we will start with some terms of how the USA looks at your relationship with your strawman corporation.

Implied Partnership. One which is not a real partnership but which is recognized by the court as such because of the conduct of the parties; in effect, the parties are estopped from denying the existence of a partnership.

Charging order. A statutorily created means for a creditor (USA) of a judgment debtor (strawman, JOHN) who is a partner of others (John) to reach the debtor's beneficial interest in the partnership (your credit), without risking dissolution of the partnership. Uniform Partnership Act, ss 28.

It is the intention of the USA, as plaintiff, to "charge" JOHN so John can go in and "conduct himself as a partner" and argue about it. You cannot "deny" or you will, of course, dishonor yourself and they win.

Premium Coaching
Covenant Group Ministries premium coaches will guide you from where you are today to where you are supposed to be tomorrow.
Virtual Coaching
Make a $50 donation to Covenantgroupministries.org using the link below for approx. an hour of Virtual Coaching.
One on One Coaching
Make a $125 donation to Covenantgroupministries.org using the link below for approx an hour of One on One Coaching.
Please contact our office at 252-364-3138 ex 104 or email us at covenantgrouptrust@gmail.com. You can also visit covenantgroupministries.org

www.ingramcontent.com/pod-product-compliance
Lightning Source LLC
Chambersburg PA
CBHW070816180526
45168CB00002B/643